On Teaching

by

Berwick Coates

Published by Berwick Coates

Publishing partner: Paragon Publishing, Rothersthorpe

© Berwick Coates 2019

The rights of Berwick Coates to be identified as the author of this work have been asserted by him in accordance with the Copyright, Designs and Patents Act of 1988.

All rights reserved; no part of this publication may be reproduced, stored in a retrieval system, or transmitted in any form or by any means, electronic, mechanical, photocopying, recording or otherwise without the prior written consent of the publisher or a licence permitting copying in the UK issued by the Copyright Licensing Agency Ltd. www.cla.co.uk

ISBN 978-1-78222-619-2

Extracts from *1066 and All That* Copyright © The Estate of Rosalind Haddon, The Estate of Jean Quick and William Yeatman. Permission granted by Methuen & Co Ltd.

Book design, layout and production management by Into Print
www.intoprint.net
+44 [0]1604 832149

Contents

Introduction and acknowledgements 4
Bella Sparrow's club 6
The fourth game 15
Heinzeit 22
It doesn't matter what you teach boys 25
Doing something 34
Greatness thrust upon them 45
A class on his own 51
Money for old rope 52
Late developer 55
Give him a big hand 59
Us don't 'ave no books, sir 69
The best policy 78
Career prospects 82
Peter Rowley and the Vikings 83
Kimber 87
Our friends, the enemy 91
Onward, Christian soldiers 99
Invigilator's notes 107
Saying thank you 110
Incident-prone 115
Back by four o'clock 121
The road to Gundagai 128
Visiting a tree 132
Second time around 138
Could do better 150
A Japanese sword 162
Doing the Reformation 166
Information in the rids 179
Expecting more 183
An extinct species 197
Are you mekkin eyes at me 213
Ordeal in the lino department 228
Taking a net 244
It takes the breath away 260
Arise, Sir Sir 277
Some progress made 285

Introduction

PEOPLE WHO, ACCORDING TO the history books, have come up with interesting observations – like Albert Einstein or Abraham Lincoln – seem to have had most opportune access to the back of an envelope just when they needed one. Just think where all those early-twentieth-century physicists would have been, or all that crowd waiting at the Gettysburg War Memorial, if envelopes and stubs of pencils had not been available.

Well, I was sitting one day with an old envelope and a pencil handy. Rest easy; I am not about to come out with a world shift in relativity, or a new paradigm in political rhetoric – just a figure. I was thinking – as one does – and fell to wondering how many lessons I had conducted in over forty years of teaching. Actually, if you calculate the gap between the date of my first lesson and the date of my last, it comes to just over fifty, but I was not in the classroom in every single year of that period. Most, but not every.

Nevertheless, I thought the exercise was one worth taking. I allowed for free periods in the week, and thirteen weeks of holiday each year. Luckily, I had enjoyed consistent good health, apart from the usual bugs, germs, and viruses, so I had missed very little. It came out to about 40,000. I had taught forty thousand lessons.

You don't survive in the classroom for forty lessons, never mind forty thousand, if you don't listen and learn, if you don't wheel and deal, if you don't see the funny side, if you don't bow and bend to the inevitable, If you don't pick up crumbs of wisdom no matter where they have fallen, if you don't have your antennae out, if you don't show willing to change while at the same time staying true to your instincts and hunches.

So I felt that I should have gathered up *something* along the way which might prove worth transmitting to others – be they pupils, parents, teachers, educationists, government ministers, or 'those who know better'. Which takes care, I fancy, of just about everybody.

Here, then, is just a dash of the flavour of what I have been up to for over forty years. It is for you to decide whether I have been wasting my time. If you think I have, please don't write to tell me; leave me to enjoy my illusions and my misconceptions.

Acknowledgements

BY THIS TIME, ANY reader of my previous books on this topic could make a fair stab at what I am going to write for this one. But that can not be helped. Things which, some say, can go without saying can go even better for being said. Mark Webb has been his usual interested, supportive, patient, and flexible self, and Yvonne Reed has, as before, been an exemplary proof-reader, checker, eagle-eye, gremlin-spotter, and commonsensical commentator. (This too in spite of a ponderous portfolio of domestic crises, alarms, excursions, and general heartache.)

Finally, I should like to add my son Stephen to this list. His contribution has gone way beyond mere filial loyalty. Interest, industry, practical knowledge of matters digital way beyond mine, to say nothing of creativity, encouragement, and balanced comment and advice. Always there.

Bella Sparrow's club

I ONCE WROTE ON a thirteen-year-old girl's report: 'School to Bella is a club where one chats to one's friends.'

The remark was not meant to be spiteful, or sarcastic, or anything particularly; I was simply trying to sum up Bella's attitude to the educational process. She was not rude, or unruly, or disruptive; she was no more idle than average, though neither was she more industrious than average; she was not ill-disposed to 'the system', or to its staff; she looked well cared-for, and she was amenable to discipline.

What was the problem then? The 'problem' was, or so it seemed to me, that Bella had long ago worked out that she had already learned from school pretty well all that was going to be of much use to her. She could read, after a fashion; she could write, after a fashion; she could spell in an approximate sort of way that was quite adequate for the prose tasks she was going to be called upon to perform in the rest of her life. She didn't need to add up; the till at Tesco's did that for her.

She was sharp enough to assess her own academic limitations, or so she thought, and decided that any further aspiration to the loftier levels of learning was going to be fraught with so much effort, with so little prospect of reward, that, frankly, the game wasn't worth the candle. The blood, sweat, and tears, and the glowing prizes, and the praise of headmasters, was for other, more gifted souls, not for her.

Well, so be it. There was plenty in life to enjoy. Her home was comfortable; her health was sound; Mum and Dad would help her to get a job in some local shop or industry or factory when the time came. Meantime there was the telly and the local disco; there was a foreign holiday to look forward to each year; and on her housing estate there was a wide circle of friends, most of whom were like-minded. In due course she would meet some likely young man, get engaged, flaunt a ring, and get married, and probably settle on the other side of the estate, and have two or three kids, just like Mum, and send them to the local comp., because that was what you did.

So what did you do at school? You did as you were told, by and large. (All credit to Mum and Dad there – manners and obedience and 'seen and not heard' and all that.) You paid a bit of attention, enough to catch the general drift. You made a stab at homework, so far as you understood what you were being asked to do. You stayed out of trouble, because it was tiresome and embarrassing, and it made you feel – well, not good.

That left quite a bit of time. So what else did you do? You chatted to your friends. And God knows, there was plenty to chat about – the most recent disco, and the hit parade; the recommendations about dress, cosmetics, boy friends, and intimate behaviour in the agony columns of the current favourite teen magazine; who's done what with whom in the bushes at the far end of the games field; the latest divorce in the avenue, and Sandra Bellingham's illegitimate baby. It passed the time admirably, and it took the mind off tiresome academic effort, most of which was semi-pointless anyway.

Now, if a thirteen-year-old girl had come to this conclusion, at this stage in her education, it would suggest that something was amiss. She was either being taught the wrong subjects, or her teachers and her school authorities were not doing their job properly. Or possibly both.

That is not to say that her teachers were either idle or stupid. They were neither, for the most part. But if a girl like Bella, and tens of thousands like her all over the country, were as switched off as this, with at least two or three years of schooling still looming in front of them – well, at the very least it makes you think.

Nor am I suggesting that the sole causes of Bella's condition are syllabus and teaching. One could point to lowest-common-denominator television programmes; to strident entertainment hammering away at the eardrums and demanding attention; to lack of ambition in the whole 'housing-estate philosophy'; to the siren sounds of advertisers extolling the virtues of a million luxuries, which, if bought, will ensure that the purchaser will be 'with it'; to magazine journalists who persuade their readers that certain habits, fashions, attitudes, and practices will ensure that the performer will be 'cool'. And so on and so on.

Of course it is easy to point out faults; it is not so easy to suggest remedies, and I am no educational philosopher. But it has often struck me that there is some serious thinking to be done by our reformers. The Bella Sparrows of the world should not be so disengaged as this.

Nor, while I am about it, should the Bruce Grubbs.

Who are the Bruce Grubbs? They are in the level lower than the Bella Sparrows. In the comprehensive school I am speaking of, Bella was in the middle 'band'. The word 'band' came about, I suspect, because they were looking for a word which did not offend, and the old word, 'stream', did. Part of the comprehensive philosophy, when it was shiny and new (years, that is, before a leading Government adviser could refer in cavalier fashion to 'your average bog standard comprehensive'), was to remove all evidence of any suggestion that children were being labelled, tagged for life. They must not be burdened with the insidious initials 'A', 'B', and 'C'. (All sorts of random codes of nomenclature were harnessed to try and 'prove' that all classes and all pupils were 'equal' in the sight of the blackboard.) The logical conclusion of this was to conduct all lessons in all subjects on the principle of mixed ability, and glowing scenarios were concocted of happy classes where the more able ones were constantly helping along their weaker brethren, who in turn nurtured in their pubertal bosoms warm gratitude for this encouragement and the ambition to be like their mentors.

It didn't work out quite like that, did it?

Sooner or later – and mostly sooner – it had to be recognised that bright children were going to be held back and slower children were going to be left behind. As somebody summed it up, 'In the old days, weaker children were put together in a separate class, where they could proceed at a roughly equal rate, and enjoy a measure of *camaraderie*. In the new mixed ability set-up, the weaker child could now see exactly how weak he was, and could measure exactly how far behind he was from the evidence of his own eyes and ears, every single day.'

There are volumes that can be written on this subject, and here is not the place to do so. I mention it only to point out that, not long after the mixed-ability gospel had been promulgated, all sorts of modifications had to be introduced in the name of common sense, not to say fairness. One of them, in our school at any rate, was to evolve three levels of general ability, based on the blindingly obvious fact that some children were of above-average ability, some were of average ability, and some were of below-average ability. In a brave attempt to avoid the label 'stream', which smacked of elitist grammar schools, it was decided to call them 'bands'. I don't think it fooled any children. As any youthful cynic well knew, you were one of three things – clever, ordinary, or thick – at least in the eyes of the educational establishment.

This was given further vindication when meetings took place at the end of each term, to decide whether certain children out in front or lagging behind in each 'band' were to be moved to a level where they could perform better or more in keeping with their proven ability, as shown in the class exams or a whole term's homework. And even here, the authorities tried desperately to avoid giving the impression that a child was being 'put up' or, worse, 'put down'. Nobody must be seen to have failed. They were called 're-allocation' meetings. All moves were sideways. Once again, I don't think the children were fooled at all.

Now let's get back to Bella and Bruce. She was, as I said, in the middle band. And she was turned off by the time she was thirteen. So what must it have been like for those in the bottom band? What was it like for, say, Bruce Grubb?

I must make clear that Bella did not necessarily represent the majority in the middle band. There were, and always have been, many, many very ordinary children who come to school, pay attention, and do their best, and they are the salt of the earth. But I maintain that there are enough Bellas to constitute a problem, the solution of which would release an appreciable amount of untapped ability and potential.

By the same token, the lowest band was not full of Bruce Grubbs, though in the nature of things it was going to be fuller than the middle one. The Bruces had discovered, probably long before the Bellas, that they were not as bright as their mates. And unless a syllabus and an approach could be devised which could offer them targets which they thought were not only achievable but worth achieving, a lot more children were going to be turned off. And they were not all going to be content with merely gazing out of the window. As one realist headmaster wrote in his report on his boarding school in the early 20th century, 'Healthy vigorous boys do not do nothing.'

Once again, I am not denigrating the efforts of countless teachers in charge of the 'lower band' classes (or – let's be blunt – 'lowest band' classes), who did, and do, sterling work. And I am not dismissing the efforts of equally large numbers of children of lesser ability who generally do their best.

But I suggest that many of these boys and girls did their best because they had been brought up to do their best, and to conform, and to behave, not because the work had been designed, and successfully, to bring the best out of them. Whether the work they were attempting was going to do them much good in the long run was another matter.

For example, I was once approached by a girl, aged fourteen, at the start of her fourth year in the secondary school, who had found that she had to make a choice (everybody always had lots of choices, another of the great merits of the comprehensives trumpeted by its advocates). The timetable was divided into several 'subject blocks', and the pupil had complete freedom to choose whatever he or she liked. In this particular 'subject block' there was a tantalising selection – something like Physics, Art, Economics, and History. Mandy was not remotely academic. I doubt if there was a single proper book in the house. She could just about read and write, and she had no conception of the world of science, aesthetics, or business. What on earth was she to do?

Bless her, she asked if she could do History. We both knew that it was making the best of a bad job. I explained to her what was involved. 'Now look, Mandy. You will find it hard, and there is a lot of writing to do. You may not understand very much of it. I can not promise that you will pass, even at a low grade. But, if you pay attention, and do your homework, and do your best, I don't mind if you get three out of ten in every test – so long, as I said, as you are doing your best. Do we have a deal?'

Yes, we had a deal. And she stuck to it. Did she pass anything? No, I don't think she did. But Mandy was never any trouble, and I knew she was doing her best.

That is not the point, though, is it? Mandy made that 'system' work because she was well-behaved, conscientious, and hardworking; it didn't 'work' because History was not the ideal choice of subject for her. History is an academic study, and she was not academic.

I don't know what went on in every comprehensive school, obviously, but my abiding impression of what was going on in mine (and mine, I reckon, was pretty typical) was that, as these less able children went up the school, the timetable seemed less and less sensibly designed to cope with their abilities, or lack of them. Far too often a class was burdened with a subject because that was the best the Director of Studies could do with the resources of staff and facilities at his disposal. Because of this recurring unsuitability, it became more and more normal for the stern disciplinarians among the staff to be put in charge of them. (Talk to any head of department when he comes to arranging who of his staff will be teaching which classes. If he is half a head of department, he will give himself the most difficult classes, and they will be in the lowest bands, because that is where you anticipate trouble.) It became, increasingly, a holding operation.

To give another example. I was once put in charge of about sixteen to twenty or so boys, aged fifteen, in the bottom class of the bottom band (a few girls too, if I remember rightly) – 5C. Or 5Z or whatever it was. It didn't matter what they called it; it was full of disillusioned teenagers who knew that they had only three more terms to survive (and the school felt the same way). And it said 'History' in the timetable.

What on earth was I to do? One period a week!

I did two things: I fell back on my own strengths, and I exploited the things that I, and they, knew they could do.

I happen to like History, and I am a bit of a ham, so I told stories – all the usual stories – about William the Conqueror, and Robin Hood, and the Battle of Agincourt, and the Spanish Armada, and – well, you follow the general idea. That took up about ten to fifteen minutes. Then I wrote on the board a brief, simple, and I hope clear, account of what I had just been saying. They copied it into their rough note books. For homework, they were to make a fair copy in their exercise books. These fair copies I collected and marked for accuracy – spelling, punctuation, and what-have-you. And I awarded marks. If time permitted, they wrote out the corrections in the next lesson.

Now these were worldly, beefy, mid-teen kids who were soon going to be earning their living in a host of pretty lowly humdrum jobs. At first, I didn't dare to hope, and I was already beginning to draw up a secondary strategy just in case.

Amazingly, it worked. They were like lambs. All right, so my discipline was sound. And they all liked system, and predictability, and routine. Like every class, regardless of age, ability, and background, they liked having something to do. And, like all children, they appreciated having their work marked, and returned – on time. So I got away with it.

But I should never have been in the position of wondering whether I was *going* to get away with it. History for one period a week is no way to cater for the educational needs of below-average pupils of fifteen.

So I come back to my point: my conclusion, after over fifteen years in this comprehensive school, was that, despite the many nice children scattered around (and of course the naughty ones) and the many conscientious teachers (and of course the lesser ones), we did not evolve a coherent strategy to cater for the pupils of lesser ability. All those years, and we hadn't made them feel that it had all been worthwhile. In effect, we sold them short.

So in some ways, it is a wonder that the Bella Sparrows and Bruce Grubbs did not get as bolshy as the real scallywags. We got away with it because of their innate good manners and tolerance. And we could hardly blame them for dealing with the situation as they saw fit. Bella chatted with her friends; Bruce did his fair share of gazing out of the window; and dear Mandy beavered away at copying up her near-incomprehensible History notes and hoped to beat the three out of ten she had got in her previous test.

The fourth game

FOR SEVERAL YEARS I was in charge of Third Form Hockey. 'Third Form', translated into modern idiom, comes out as 'Year 9'. In plain English, 13-14-year-olds. In the grammar school in which I was working, that meant arranging games every Thursday afternoon for just over eighty boys.

We had four members of staff allocated for this. That meant four games. You needed eleven a side for a proper game. So three games were the obvious starting-point. That took care of sixty-six boys. Allowing for routine absentees, there might be anything from about twelve to eighteen left.

Since we were concerned to provide not only athletic exercise but instruction in the game of hockey, it followed that one needed to organise games for players of roughly equal skill, in order to stretch them. So, naturally, we had a 'first game' and a 'second game' and a 'third game'. As boys showed signs of improvement or decline we could move them from one game to another in following weeks. It provided interest and incentive. It gave the coaches flexibility too. For instance, if a coach suspected that a boy in, say, the second game might turn out to be a better defender than attacker, he could try him out in the third game, to see how he performed. If the experiment worked, he could then promote him back to the second game the next week.

That left the remaining twelve to eighteen. There were not enough to make a full two-team game, so the teacher did what he could with the rump. Every so often, in the name of fairness, the teacher in charge

– me – would invert the whole thing. Put the weakest players in the first game, slightly stronger performers in the second game, and so on, right down to the fourth, which would contain the bright sparks. But an afternoon with only about fourteen of them gave the chance to practise all sorts of moves and manoeuvres not possible in a full game. It could be quite intensive coaching. And everybody else got a fair crack of the whip in a proper, full, eleven-a-side game.

However, the average, the usual thing, the norm, was three games in descending order of talent, with the non-benders coagulated in the bottom game. When the notice went up on the board, I usually substituted the word 'fourth', in an effort to cater for sporting sensibilities among the less talented brethren. As a change, I might write 'Extras' or 'Reserves'. It fooled nobody. With that unnerving knack for ruthless precision, for calling a spade a spade (or even a bloody shovel), which is the birthright of every schoolboy, this bottom game was universally known as the 'Chuckouts'.

(Years later I was working in another school which instituted a system of small cards to be awarded for particular virtue, usually in academic work, but sometimes for other things as well. They were to be known as 'merit cards'. Within a week or two, they had entered pupil vernacular as 'creep cards'. But still, however, thought of as worth the effort.)

The 'Chuckouts' nomenclature became so common that teachers found themselves using the term as well, with no insult implied or involved, simply as a convenient term of reference. It was a bit like the position of the Quakers. Originally used as an insult by their enemies, the term was taken on board by the Quakers themselves, and used thereafter with pride.

Well, it was like that with the Chuckouts. They evolved their own culture, their own ethos. Not just anybody could become a Chuckout. You had to be well below a recognised level of aptitude. You were never selected to play for your house. You never bulged with a single muscle. On the field of play, you never ran when you could walk, and you never walked when you could stand still. You never neglected an opportunity to sit down when the teacher wasn't looking.

You could tell a Chuckout by glancing at him. For a start, he didn't look like a hockey player. It was a red-letter day if he remembered to bring his kit at all, and his forgetfulness was usually the result not of ill will or unco-operativeness but of sheer inefficiency and (often scholarly) absent-mindedness. We had one boy, who must remain nameless, who forgot his games kit nearly every week for two terms. When he did finally remember to bring his hockey gear, the cricket season had started.

A Chuckout took longer to get changed than everyone else. He had more thumbs on each hand than anybody else. He had no muscles; his arms fell like tubular bells out of baggy sleeves, and his legs shot straight out of enormous shorts into floppy socks and knubbly boots with large bows on the laces. He didn't bulge anywhere; he stuck out – elbows, collar bones, ribs, knees. His nose was red and his wrists were blue. His shoulders were permanently hunched against whatever elements a capricious Providence had inflicted for that afternoon. His face was the colour of ivory and he often wore moon-shaped spectacles. His stick was too long and too heavy, and, for all the familiarity he seemed to have with it, it might have been a halberd. It was often used like one.

He had no bounce, no dash, no agility, no strength, no stamina, and no co-ordination. (The apogee of this total lack of ability was reached in a cricket games session in the summer, when a colleague, afraid that if he tossed the ball to a boy it might injure him, actually walked up to him and placed the ball in his hand – and he dropped it.)

It followed therefore that learning the basic skills of hockey was going to be quite beyond him. He could not bully off, because he could not co-ordinate three separate pairs of movements with the stick. Attempts at hitting propelled several ounces of mud and dirt in the direction of the opposition far more often than it did the ball. Attempts at stopping produced a bent, buttock-bulging stance and the tentative extension of the stick along the ground in the million-to-one hope that there might be some kind of magnetism that would somehow bring the ball into contact with the crook. The position was not unlike that of a small boy trying to fish a wayward paper boat out of a pond. To be fair to him, these were the days of universal grass pitches, which were a good deal more unpredictable than the modern artificial surfaces with their billiard-table precision.

Flicking the ball was quite out of the question – an esoteric practice of transcendental complexity for the likes of demigods. A Chuckout evolved a grip all his own, which placed the hands miles apart, or the wrong way round. As a variant, he developed a one-handed style that possessed a loose, disjointed, random charm which defied classification.

It followed in turn that teaching the principles of positional play was like trying to convey the differential calculus to a classroom of innumerates. By comparison, herding cats would have been child's play.

However, they did cotton on to one thing. They grasped the elemental fact that the object of the game was to propel the ball towards the net of the opposition's goal, and they duly set about this quite enjoyable task so far as their physique and talents permitted – all together, at the same time, and all the time. It produced an engaging variant of the Eton Wall Game, only more deadly on account of the weapons. Goalies were pretty thin on the ground. There were rarely more than thirteen or fourteen players anyway. If the Eton Wall Game scrum showed signs of approaching the defenders' circle – like a drunken, multi-limbed insect – the master in charge would place himself in the necessary strategic position. The aforesaid scrum normally proceeded at such a glacial pace that it was quite possible, with very little expenditure of energy, for the master to play goalie at both ends, and still have enough breath to blow his whistle. The ball was moreover propelled so slowly that there was little physical danger to him.

The amazing thing was that many of these dashing sportsmen actually enjoyed their hockey, and they created many original ways of entertaining themselves. Free hits and flying divots were occasions of great amusement; indeed, when they were not actually engaged in the Eton Wall Game, it was a favourite pastime for a couple of unemployed full-backs to amuse themselves by seeing who could despatch the greater number of these divots at each other – till the irate master unsportingly put a stop to it. Empty pop bottles left behind the backboard of the goal testified to a full-back's fondness for a quick snort when things were a bit quiet.

Now and again, a full-back would be taken by surprise by a most uncharacteristic burst of speed on the part of the Wall Game. I remember one being interrupted in his divot-shifting by the sudden sound of jostling sticks and cheery voices. Not a whit abashed, he turned, straightened up, shouted 'look out, chaps – the enemy' to nobody in particular, and prepared for battle.

Luckily, injuries were comparatively rare, because the ball was seldom propelled with sufficient velocity to endanger a babe in arms. It was the uncontrolled sticks that were the danger. They were often swung like tomahawks, and a group of embattled opponents all searching for the ball could look, and sound, like a bunch of Apaches on the warpath.

Because of the funereal pace, actual events were a rarity. The ball hardly ever left the field of play, unless dredged in that direction by the combined dragging effect of fifteen sticks and thirty boots. The master soon learned not to blow his whistle for every infringement of the rules, because he would have run out of breath long before his charges would have exhausted their capacity for illegality. A goal, if and when it came, was celebrated as if it were the Relief of Mafeking.

One particular skill the Chuckouts did develop, though, was prolonging half-time. They reckoned that by then they all deserved a rest. And the longer they could spin out half-time, the less would be the exertion needed in the shorter second half. So they would all lend a hand to engage the teacher in animated conversation. It was amazing how many minutes you could tick away if you worked at it.

It was from one of these extended half-times that a remark comes down the years. It encapsulates the Chuckouts' sense of humour, sense of fun, cheerful disregard of the finer points of the game (indeed, of any points of the game), and determination to enjoy it on their own terms.

A group of them had gathered round me, obviously to sustain me in general badinage and chat while the minutes quietly evaporated. One of them dug his hand into a capacious pocket of his baggy blue shorts.

'Like a sweet, sir?'

'Why, that's very kind of you. Yes. I will. Thanks.'

It was a make unknown to me.

To keep the party going, I said, 'Very nice. What are they?'

'Sex pills, sir.'

Heinzeit

CHILDREN OFTEN GET IT wrong. And it is not their fault. They listen to what their elders say, and the fact that they repeat it shows firstly that they really were listening, and secondly that they thought what they heard to be worth repeating. These two – well, compliments if you like – are often forgotten in the wave of laughter that is brought about by their mistake.

The mistake comes about not because of their lack of intelligence, and, as we have just shown, certainly not because of their lack of attentiveness, but obviously because of their lack of knowledge and experience. They simply have so little to go on.

I, for example, at the age of six, was quite sure that the item that all ladies carried wherever they went was a 'hambag'. How did I know that? Because that's what they always called it. Again, when I used to hear the Lord's Prayer recited in our assembly hall at my first primary school, I derived great consolation from the fact that the Almighty had made provision for the survival of the male sex – 'for ever and ever are men'. It did not bother me that He had not made similar provision for the survival of the other one. (I was a chauvinist at five – how awful. And who or what was responsible for that?)

Similarly a man of my acquaintance was firmly convinced at five that God had a Christian name. Why? Because everybody started the prayer with 'Our Father, which art in Heaven, Harold be thy name'.

And this kind of mistake is not confined to the reception class, or even the middle juniors. Anybody, right up to a leaving age of 18, can get it wrong, and their error is often the result of attentiveness, not inattentiveness.

Some years ago, I was in the habit of pointing out to my 'A' Level History classes that historians have it easy. They come along after the events they describe, often centuries after those events, and, thanks to their extensive, and intensive, research, they accumulate a vast amount of knowledge about that period, or that century, or that decade, or whatever. They can often end up knowing more about, say, London in the 1770's, than people who actually lived in the London of the 1770's. They can home in on errors in the behaviour of the people whose actions they chronicle; they can pontificate; they can pass judgment. It can, if not checked, result in a diminution of the people whose lives are being recorded. The historian can easily lose sight of the fact that a man in London in the 1770's was human and short of knowledge, and was liable to make mistakes even when he was doing his best.

All this, I said, and frequently, was because of hindsight. It is easy to be wise after the event, and historians love being wise. Well, everybody does.

One of my class had obviously been taking in all this, and, in her next essay, I found reference to a curious phenomenon called *heinzeit*. This is a splendid example of the mistake which is not only perfectly understandable, and of course funny, but absolutely charming as well.

Becky had not only been listening; she had understood; she had chosen the exact context in which to quote it; and, having decided, from its Teutonic sound, that it was German, had supplied a perfectly plausible German spelling. More than that; she had appreciated that, in the world of history and criticism, one often used foreign words and phrases – say, *fait accompli*, *coup d'état*, *pièce de résistance*, *tour de force*, *chargé d'affaires*, and so on. So she had decided, very intelligently, to drop a foreign word of her own into the proceedings – and, as I said, in perfect context. It was not only charming; it was endearing.

So the teacher had his quiet and gratified chuckle. But it deserved more mileage than that. The problem was, how to exploit it. And here a teacher has to be oh, so careful. Ridicule, as everyone knows, can eat at the very soul of a pupil.

The trick was not to *make* the joke, but to *share* it. To show that the error would not diminish the pupil but enhance the lesson for the whole class. And this could not be done where the class did not have confidence in the teacher. Here I shall venture to claim credit for having created some. My judgment told me that, if I presented this in the right way, Becky would join in the joke.

I explained that, once in a while, one came across an error which not only deserved to be right far more than the truth, but which graced and adorned a lesson in its scholarliness and delicacy. And which was so rare and esoteric – *was ist das Heinzeit?* I was pleased, and relieved, to see that Becky laughed as much as anybody else, and she never, so far as I know, held it against me.

All right, so I was lucky; I got away with it. My judgment could, I suppose, have been proved wrong. Becky could have folded up for weeks. But she didn't. The incident was a fine example of the maxim that perhaps the greatest thing a teacher needs to build is not the habit of industry, or neatness, or thoroughness, or inquisitiveness, or sheer peace and quiet, but trust. If they trust you, you are in business. If they don't, you're not, and it doesn't matter how clever you are.

It doesn't matter what you teach boys

When I was at my grammar school, I studied Latin for seven years, and Greek for four.

Very few people, I fancy, can claim that nowadays. Both subjects are so out of fashion that it is unlikely that many would *claim* it even if they had. They might even hesitate to *admit* it, unless they followed it up with disclaimers and provisos and extenuating circumstances, as if to prove that it wasn't their fault that their education was so out of touch with reality and modernity.

But it's fashion, isn't it? Latin and Greek were simply two more victims of changing taste, and the world of education is no more immune to the pressures of changing taste than any other world. When schools began to appear in significant numbers in the nineteenth century, the world of learning was dominated by the Classics – Latin and Greek. It was not a question of being 'right' or 'wrong'; they just 'were'. The modern world owed its heritage to the Middle Ages, which had kept alive the lamp of learning in a thousand years of troublous times by means of Greek and Latin – especially Latin. They were the only avenues, the only media of scholarship. Add the stranglehold of the Christian Church on man's thinking processes, and it is hardly surprising that these subjects continued to dominate.

In the absence of a national educational system, there seemed to be little reason to make radical changes. Only wealthy and privileged people received any kind of education (private tutors or Flashman public schools) beyond the three R's, and when they did it was usually Latin, Greek, and the Bible. Small wonder that MP's could quote from the Roman and Greek authors, in the original, in their parliamentary speeches, and expect to be understood, even appreciated.

When it became likely that bigger numbers of children were going to be put into schools, especially secondary schools, there arose the question of what to teach them. The authorities had never before been faced with the problem of what to do, on a national scale, with young people, in large numbers, concentrated in one room for considerable periods of time. Almost instinctively, those who reckoned that they knew best decided to carry on teaching what had always been taught. And if children were so rash or unreasonable as to show reluctance or, worse, rebellion, they were to be beaten. After all, that was what had always gone on in private households in every class of society. There was no other way.

These things take a long time to die. There are plenty of men alive today who will boast not only that they were regularly beaten when they were at school, but that they didn't think it had done them any harm. (Perhaps it hadn't; who knows?)

All right, so Latin and Greek were 'there', like Everest. They dominated the curriculum. But it may come as a surprise to discover the *extent* to which they dominated the curriculum. In my work as a school archivist, I discovered, in a school report as late as the early 1920's, that English (which any British educationist, of whatever political colour, would accept today as a basic component of the timetable) was not a regular part of it then. Shortly after the Great War, it 'came in' as an alternative to Latin. Indeed, such was the school's sense of thrift that on the report forms, the word 'Latin' was still there, and, if a pupil chose to do English, the 'Latin' was crossed out by hand and 'English' substituted. And I darkly suspect that the change occurred not because the boy in question showed a sudden passion for his native tongue, but because he was considered too thick to continue Latin profitably.

As with discipline, the authorities had no previous experience. They could think of no way to convey learning other than by rote. They had large numbers of children in a room, most of whom had no particular desire to be there. What else could they do but drills and exercises, blackboard and bash, pain and cane?

These of course are generalisations. Not all schools or teachers behaved as I have described, and fresh subjects – Maths, Science, Geography, History, and so on – did make their way into the timetable.

But habits, like ideas, die hard. It took a long time for teachers of the old days to wonder whether all children might not be potential rebels, philistines, and iconoclasts. They are, of course, and always will be, but the educational world has slowly grasped that there are ways round their rebellion, philistinism, and iconoclasm. They don't always have to be met head on. They can be led as well as driven, motivated as well as drilled, inspired as well as frightened.

The trouble with Latin and Greek was that they were so full of tenses and cases and moods and agreements and conjugations. Lists, charts, tables. That was the snag with being dead. They had congealed. Had there been some societies somewhere which still *spoke* ancient Latin and Greek, the languages would have still been developing, and it would have been fun to try and keep up with the latest colloquialisms. But Latin and Greek were, as I said, just 'there', and you had to lump it.

As you grow up, assuming you are willing to be fair about them, you begin to see that both languages have great value – not necessarily in helping you to speak them, because nobody does. But they are, between them, the windows on to the whole culture and heritage of Europe for the past two and half thousand years. The better you know Latin and Greek, and the societies from which they sprang, the more Europe makes sense.

However, you can't expect schoolboys to understand all this. In their world, you had to do Latin five times a week, and that was that. And, if you chose to take up Greek, you did *that* five times a week as well. Well, I did.

In case you are wondering why any boy with sense would choose to add to his miseries by taking up a second classical subject, I have to admit to quite selfish reasons. I cannot answer for the others in our set, but I wouldn't mind betting that some of them were like me. It was quite simple; I was a bit of a swot. I could actually remember those endless lists of verbs and tenses and pronouns – quite easily, it appeared. I was therefore getting good marks for homeworks and exercises and exams. The logic seemed inescapable: if I could get good marks for Latin, I ought to be able to get good marks for Greek. QED.

That didn't mean that I *liked* it necessarily. What I liked about it was the success. But other boys, I could see, were not so successful, and so were disposed to like it less.

However, that was missing the point so far as the advocates of the Classics were concerned, indeed the advocates of any kind of early education. Education was there to do you good, like castor oil. Liking it had nothing to do with it. The mission of those early teachers (and the tradition died hard) was to make you get on with it. Just as you were brought up to fear the Victorian father, so you usually finished up fearing the Victorian teacher. Children, it was felt, had to be made to mind – to be God-fearing, father-fearing, school-fearing, and pretty well everything else-fearing.

By the mid-twentieth century, these attitudes had naturally lost their sharp edges, but it is fair to say that schoolboys as a breed did not exactly have a soft spot for Latin or Greek.

I was lucky in that I was taught by a succession of remarkable Latin teachers, and one Greek teacher, who understood this. Mr. McIver made us get on with it, and we took no liberties. Mr. Forge was matter-of-fact, no-nonsense, and practical, but he too got on with it, and we appreciated his professionalism. Mr. Cripps, a teacher of rare humanity, actually got some laughs out of it.

But the man who had the greatest influence – for me, at any rate – was Mr. Brown. As I was taught both Latin and Greek by him for four years each, in sheer man hours – what is today known as pupil contact time – it would have been surprising if I had *not* been influenced by him.

I have written about him at greater length elsewhere (see *Starkeye and Co.*), but the one feature of his teaching I want to draw attention to here is this business of liking the thing. He knew boys didn't like Latin and Greek. I don't think he particularly expected them to – well, not at first anyway. Later, when we were in the Sixth Form, we began to become aware of other dimensions to the subject beyond automatic learning and memorising.

But Mr. Brown did not apologise for his subject. He

knew, with passionate conviction, that what he taught – the Classics – was important. He was convinced that the study of Latin and Greek was the finest training for the mind yet devised by the human brain. The benefits would come later; small boys were not expected to see that. How could they?

Mr. Brown understood full well that he taught subjects that were difficult and unpopular. What healthy boy clapped his hands at the prospect of yet more irregular verbs and subjunctives? In dead languages.

Out of this arose his philosophy, which he put to us in a Sixth Form lesson. *A propos* of something I have now forgotten, he threw away the remark, 'It doesn't matter what you teach boys so long as they don't like it.'

I don't suggest that it was a carefully-considered, definitive summary of his educational philosophy. No – there was a lot more to Mr. Brown than that. But it did illustrate his shrewdness, his realism, his dry sense of humour, and his understanding of the boyish mentality. (He never had the opportunity to teach girls.) The remark was typical of the sort of titbit which any experienced, well-rounded teacher might throw out to a senior class with calculated casualness, knowing that it's not the main meal that they usually gobble up but the scraps.

'It doesn't matter what you teach boys so long as they don't like it.'

I expect he meant small boys – say, up to about thirteen or fourteen. After that age, we noticed that his manner slowly changed, and increasingly he took off the lid and showed us the works – revealed depths and subtleties and complexities and general riches which changed the whole aspect of both Latin and Greek. But my point is still valid;

you had to flog through an awful lot of stodge before you got there.

And that 'flogging', in the long run, was no bad thing – that was what he was saying. You can't expect to like everything that comes your way; every job before you is not going to be a bowl of cherries. But you owe it to the job, and to yourself, to make the best you can of it. And – as often as not – by a sort of back-handed logic, the process generates a satisfaction which can come close, on occasions, to actual liking, if only in retrospect.

Put another way, progress which comes easily is barely noticed, much less appreciated; progress which comes only after prolonged struggle is much more valued. A good teacher (regardless of subject) could help to imbue you with the character to stick at it. That is where the satisfaction and pride come from. It is not only the 'struggle' either; it is the 'prolonged' dimension too which counts. You not only have to grapple; you have to grapple over an extended period.

Look at the wild emotions exhibited by athletes and skaters and cup-winning footballers. Yes, perhaps they do look excessive to us in our armchairs, but then we haven't spent months, perhaps years, on a programme of training and early mornings and self-denial and rigid discipline, all with just one goal in view, to be determined by only an hour or so of explosive effort – in some cases only a few seconds. It is simply satisfaction. Somewhat vigorous satisfaction, maybe, but satisfaction nevertheless.

Well, Latin verbs could be a bit like that. Those athletes, I'm sure, did not *enjoy* every training session at the pool or the track or the stadium, at unsocial hours, month after month, any more than we enjoyed endless conjugations and making adjectives agree with nouns and remembering to put the verb at the end. But the discipline was something you don't forget, and it reveals to you a little of what you are capable of. It can bring things out of you that you didn't know were there. If it hadn't been for that unwelcome task, you would never have found out.

Some years later, when I joined the Army (not voluntarily, I hasten to add – this was National Service), inevitably I came up against the great feature of military life which everybody, absolutely everybody, thinks they know about – square-bashing. Drill. On the parade ground. At ease – attention – left turn – right turn – about turn – quick march – slow march – right form – left form – close order – open order. Just when you think you have mastered all that, the Army weighs in with another avalanche of commands, based on the handling of the rifle – order arms – slope arms – present arms – port arms. . . . And so on and so on and so on. And everything so damned loud – bawled commands – stamping the feet – slapping the rifle.

What recruit in his right mind would *like* it? Cold mornings, freezing fingers, pulled muscles, abusive corporals, wayward rifles, tight boots. But I have to tell you that, after several weeks, we found ourselves taking an interest. We would never have believed it. By the time of our passing-out parade at the end of training, we *wanted* to do well; we *wanted* to get our movements crisp and sharp and together, as a united squad; we *wanted* to make a noise slapping the rifle; we *wanted* to look good for the spectators; we *wanted* the approval of our drill sergeant.

So our drill sergeant and Mr. Brown were both on to a great truth: it was no great achievement to win laurels at something you enjoyed; but to win them at a task you didn't like – now that really *was* something.

Doing something

MANY OF US, IF we are lucky, make the acquaintance, early in our chosen work, whatever the activity, of a mentor figure. In my case it was teaching. This 'mentor' may not be actively coaching you, or even keeping an unofficial eye on you. Young teachers didn't have 'mentors' when I started. The country was so short of teachers that the authorities simply threw them into the classroom and hoped for the best. They certainly couldn't spare other teachers to watch over them in their free periods. In the school where I started, I don't think there were any such things as free periods. At any rate I don't remember them. A beginner just got on with it – though you were required to submit for examination, each week, your proposed schedule of lessons for every class on every day. The headmaster had to find time to check them, when he didn't have free periods either, because he was his own secretary.

In this sink-or-swim environment, a young teacher had little to turn to in the way of human reference book, or even book reference book if it comes to that. If he had a grain of common sense, therefore, he kept his eyes open for the better practitioners, and learned from them.

Luckily, most schools have them. Not lording it; not flashing the stripes on their sleeve; not burdening you with ponderous or glib advice (there are some of the last type of course, but you soon learn to spot them and treat their comments for what they are worth). No – they are simply around. You notice them, often not so much for the things they do as the things they don't do. Their stillness, their silences, their lack of rush. You watch them. You take note of their skill, their experience, and their approach to the things which crop up in an average working day. You come to envy their *sang froid*, their unflappability, their sense of perspective, often their sense of humour too. And you marvel at their pupil control.

You listen to them. Shrewd judgments, searching questions, sharp comments, relevant anecdotes, are all pretty thick on the ground where they have casually thrown them, easily placed for a watchful junior to pick up.

It so happened that the man who did that for me was in fact the headmaster – well, the new headmaster. When I started at this school, in November, they were so short of teachers in the city that we didn't even have a headmaster. The deputy head was running the show. The 'proper' headmaster did not appear till the beginning of the Easter term. What had caused the hiatus I never found out.

Anyway, the new man appeared early in January. It was a quiet start. He said only a few words at his first assembly. All I remember was his tentative hope that, as the school was called 'All Saints', that was what he hoped we would all be.

I don't think for one moment that he actually envisaged a great lift in the moral lives of the inmates. I soon discovered that he was far too great a realist for that. It was a joke, a gentle comment on the fact that we are all only too human. It was my first indication of his wry humour – a blend of gentle optimism that teachers might be able to do a spot of good along the line, coupled with a tolerant understanding that all children are well endowed with their share of original sin. In effect an acceptance that we were never going to make them 'all saints', but it was still worth the effort to give them a little shove in the right direction.

Bill Johnson did not look dynamic. He was not large; he was not athletic; he walked with a slight stoop; he wore glasses, and peered. He had a slightly reedy tenor voice, and a slow, ruminative, rural-philosopher delivery which compelled attention. He had served in the War, so was no innocent. However, he was not one of those veterans who never lost an opportunity tell you that he had seen some service. You just found out somehow, and anyway it showed. You couldn't rattle him. Well, I never saw him rattled.

After three years at university and another two in the Army (National Service), I reckoned my education was pretty jolly comprehensive. There are few creatures wronger than young men who think they have seen it all. The next eight or nine months opened my eyes and my mind; they were in fact another complete education for me. Thank God I learned fast. It was a case of having to if you wanted to survive. And Bill Johnson presided over my apprenticeship. Like all good superiors, he noticed many more things about you than inferiors gave him credit for. Perhaps he thought I had some promise, I don't know. But I am sure he saw me for exactly what I was – a bright enough young fellow, with plenty of energy, but with a *great* deal to learn.

He never formally took me on one side and offered me 'training', or even informal 'help' – they would call it 'counselling' today, I suppose. But he dropped endless little remarks, sometimes to my face, sometimes to the world at large, all of which I found perceptive, useful, and, on my frequent bad days, a great encouragement.

For example, one lunch-hour, during 'dinner duty'

(we were always doing dinner duty, it seemed), we were chatting about this and that, and he must have noticed that I was looking a bit glum, after some *contretemps* or other with a recalcitrant pupil, and had slipped into the mood which convinced me that I was simply not getting through. Perhaps I had built it up into something worse, a sort of complex – you know, my whole approach was different from theirs, we were chalk and cheese, and however hard I tried, I was never going to influence them at all – and all young teachers like to feel that they are 'influencing' their charges.

He peered up at me (as I said, he was not a very big man), sucked his teeth, and said, 'You know, you mustn't worry about the fact of where you've been. These children don't get much opportunity to rub shoulders with a graduate from Cambridge University. [It was a tough school in a tough area in a gritty northern city]. A lot is rubbing off you on to them of which you have no wot and of which they have no wot.' I liked his literary use of 'wot'.

I felt better for that.

It was an education, too, to watch him dealing with awkward children, and, for that matter, awkward parents. This usually happened on Wednesdays.

Wednesdays he set aside for administration and 'matters arising' – in effect, discipline. Many schools like ours were so short of facilities that we did not enjoy the luxury of a school secretary. Bill did his own secretarial work in a lofty, poky garret up a minuscule staircase beside the main hall. Government circulars, local government bumf, reports of visiting inspectors, staff work schemes, staff salaries, union correspondence, kitchen accounts, attendance registers, parents' letters (not, fortunately, very numerous, because most of our parents were not very literary-minded, and in any case they much preferred to come in and have it out face to face – so perhaps it was not so 'fortunately' after all) – all these things, and many more, dropped on to his crowded desk, and took up most of Wednesday morning.

Wednesday afternoon he gave up, when the situation demanded it, and it usually did, to what he called his detective work. A lot of this stemmed from absenteeism. Checking that absence notes were genuine. We had school attendance officers to go round and actually knock on doors. He built an impressive portfolio of these notes, so that he could compare the writing in them later when a persistent absentee negligently presented yet another 'note from Mum' which did not tally with the previous ones. Another give-away, of course, was spelling. Even Mum could usually spell words like 'cough' or, at a pinch, 'indigestion', but it was often beyond the vocabulary of the criminal fraternity.

Another problem was ensuring that end-of-term reports reached home. I once found one such document in tiny pieces in the gutter right outside the school. Its owner was so disgusted at it, or so fearful of what might happen if it reached home, that he couldn't get rid of it quickly enough, and did not even take the precaution of destroying out of sight further up the road.

Bill was a great believer in this amassing of evidence. One of his greatest coups, I thought, was the nailing of Jennifer Seaman. Our Jennifer, who was growing up much faster than her calendar years, was one of those girls who hated physical education and abhorred swimming. We were not able to send batches of children to the swimming baths every week, so it was difficult to keep track. Our

Jennifer homed in on this loophole, and regularly played what she thought was her trump card every time she was scheduled for the local baths. This was a note from her mother to the effect that it was the time of Jennifer's monthly period, and that therefore could she be excused.

Male teachers in those days were a lot more uncomfortable about feminine hygiene than they are now. People generally simply did not talk about such things. I was comfortably into my teens before I discovered that my mother *had* periods. This reticence spilled over into one's later dealings with female pupils, and the little minxes shamelessly traded on it. Mention periods, and young male teachers could fold up and give you anything you wanted.

Well, the Jennifer Seamans of this world met their match with Bill Johnson. Again, he patiently collected his evidence, scruffy note by scruffy note. After about a term of Jennifer's wriggling, and excuses, and parent's letters, he was able to present a meticulously-documented case of a very rare teenage girl who had apparently menstruated no fewer than seven times in three months.

With difficult parents the technique was different. I wonder whether he had ever practised judo, where the 'player' is taught to use the attacker's own momentum against himself. Bill rarely argued; he listened. He let them make the running. I once watched him do this.

Having a row can be a most enjoyable business. Particularly if you have come steaming into the school determined to 'have it out' with the Headmaster. It is disconcerting to be met, not with a return of fire, but with total silence. Worse, with complete and very watchful attention. The silence, after a while, becomes almost unnerving, and the usual effect is for the boarding party to dry up.

(Incidentally, this silence can be equally unnerving for a teacher in a classroom. Every once in a while, you are doing something, or explaining something, or telling a story, and you suddenly sense that they are quiet – totally quiet. You realise, with a thrill almost of horror, that they are listening. Not just lending an ear, but *listening*, with every antenna stretched. And not just taking it all in, but dying to hear what you are going to say next. And you think, 'My God, how can I live up to this? How can I keep it up?' It shakes you. Fortunately, it doesn't happen very often.)

Well, Bill did this with Mrs. Harrison. When she had finished what she had to say about the school, and the staff, and the unfairness of the rules, and the bad treatment of her son, and anything else she could think of while she was about it, he leaned back in his chair, turned, reached out towards a cubby-hole in his desk, selected a local education office form, laid it on his desk, and picked up his pen.

'Now then, Mrs. Harrison, which school would you like me to transfer your son to?'

'Ah, well, Mr. Johnson – I mean – well, not exactly – I mean to say – I were only – um – '

Within minutes Mrs. Harrison was on her way home, and Master Harrison was going to have to take his punishment after all.

So I looked and I learned. Bill could also let slip the occasional observation which could do the ego quite a bit of good.

The last Friday in the month was always especially welcome. Not because it was Friday (though 'TGIF' was a hackneyed teachers' mantra – 'thank God it's Friday'), but because it was pay day. The machinery then was a lot more primitive than it is now. Nowadays we receive in our pigeon-holes sophisticated printed sheets as complicated as the orders for the Normandy landings. In those days the education office sent a single foolscap page of perforated paper to the school, itemising in one single line the details of each teacher's salary and tax for that month. Bill would tear them all off, and go walkabout round the school, bearing the relevant slender slip for each member of staff. (Again, imagine headmasters doing this office-boy stuff today.)

It is a suitable juncture to slip in the story of the infant teacher who had a crowd of tiny acolytes sitting on the floor round her feet, listening to a story, when the head came in with the fragile but welcome fiscal fragment. When he had gone, somebody asked her what it was.

'That,' she explained, 'is the piece of paper which tells me how much my pay is. My wages.'

This created a murmur of interest. One minute interlocutor piped up.

'Where do you work then, Miss?'

Well, one Friday afternoon, Bill came in with my pay slip. By good fortune, they were copying some History notes from the board. A class of ten-year-olds. I had at least advanced in teaching technique sufficiently to have tumbled to the fact that the later in the week, and the later in the afternoon, that you are working, the more it behoves you to provide work that is suitably absorbing and routine, so as not to provide opportunities for creative mischief. So on a Friday afternoon, it was vital. If they are busy enough, they don't get around to thinking up trouble. And children love copying.

I had also learnt a good lesson from the Army: if you have men under your control, you will only keep that control if you keep them busy. Hence the adage about digging holes and filling them in again. But it's true; you can't beat busy-ness.

So there they were, with nothing on show but the tops of heads.

Bill gave me my slip, looked round the room, leaned back slightly, and peered up at me.

'Y'know, one of the things I like about your room is that, when I come in here, they are always doing something.'

A powerful lesson. And a welcome encouragement. I treasured both.

Finally, a minute masterclass in perspective. The best practitioners in any activity have the trick of encapsulating a particular process or problem in such a way that you understand it much better, you feel better equipped to deal with it, and, as often as not, you are smiling at the same time.

We had a large family at our school. In fact, we had several large families. Many of our local inhabitants did not allow their often narrow houses, their narrow finances, and their narrow prospects, to interfere with their fertility. And they could show remarkable creativity too in the way they catered for these urges. We discovered one household where the boys (nice boys too – and well behaved) were only half-brothers. The father had a wife and a mentally backward sister-in-law both under his roof, and favoured them alternately with his conjugal attentions.

But there were several 'ordinary' families too, each one of them liable to provide much for the authorities to think about – shoplifting, breaking and entering, neighbour-harassing, absenteeism (naturally, otherwise they wouldn't have found the time for the crime). They were regular customers for the 'nit lady' – the visiting nurse. (This was one of the many sharp lessons I learned; I had thought lice had gone out with Charles Dickens and the Artful Dodger.) The investigations about cloakroom theft regularly stopped with them. Theirs were the parents who invariably failed to turn up for parents' evening. It was their activities which prompted visits to the school from the local constabulary – another item in Bill's crowded Wednesdays.

There was one dynasty in particular which was a miniature crime wave all by itself. Let us call them the Wainwrights. (I apologise to the many Wainwright families who are spotless upholders of the law, but I have to call them something, and whatever name I used I should have to make this apology.)

In the top class was our Georgie. Smoking, drinking under age, shoplifting, appearances in magistrates' courts, and a spell in reform school to round it off. Below him came our Doreen. Drunk and disorderly, perpetual absenteeism, a beefy boy-friend in the Merchant Navy, and a darkly-suspected abortion. Then there was our Vincent, regular bookie's runner and purveyor of cigarettes to juniors in the playground. After him came our Rita, who had not yet graduated much beyond smoking in the toilets, but who had secured for herself a nineteen-year-old spiv boy-friend with a loud kipper tie. So she had definite potential.

That did not take into consideration our Walter, who had left two years before, and who had already done two spells in boot camp, and was on probation; and Father, who was, at the time of going to press, currently detained at Her Majesty's pleasure in Wakefield.

Last, bottom of the pile, was our Albert. Eleven years old. Scruffy. Mischievous. Needed watching. But not nasty. In fact, quite likeable. He got on well with the teachers. He always had a cheery smile, and he sat in class with no ill feeling. Did a bit of work from time to time. No Einstein, but no trouble. You felt that, given some luck and the right circumstances, you might be able to do something with him. He was, so far, the only member of the family who had not been up before a beak, a bench, or a Borstal committee.

Of course the family dice were loaded against him, though he didn't know it yet.

Bill Johnson summed it up with beautiful, wry precision.

He sucked his teeth one day, and gazed at nobody in particular.

'You know what? Young Albert Wainwright is asking himself one question: "Does crime pay?"'

Greatness thrust upon them

I suppose I should have seen something coming; both of them had beaming smiles on their faces.

'Ah, there you are, sir.'

'Yes?' Well, I couldn't deny it, could I? And once they had secured the first admission, they were well on their way.

'Can you spare a minute, sir?'

Mid-morning break. Standing in a corridor outside the Common Room. And I had just paused to agree with them. How could I possibly claim that I could not spare a single minute? They had scored their second point.

And of course I was tangentially curious. I hadn't taught either of them for at least two years, and they had not made what you could call a deep impression. I remembered their names – Lewin and Traill – and that was about all. I knew next to nothing about their careers after they left my tutelage. We might have been in different orbits for all we saw of each other. It is a common legend among those outside school life – that is, nearly everybody – that all the teachers see all the pupils all the time. Schools can be remarkably compartmentalised; rigid timetables dictate that everybody has to follow narrowly-prescribed avenues.

So what did Messrs. Lewin and Traill want?

'Well, sir, we were thinking – that is, we were wondering – [a certain amount of foot-shuffling] – if – [a deep breath before the final plunge] – if you would consent to becoming president of the new society we'd like to form.'

School societies break out from time to time like a sort of rash, and are nursed, tolerated, allowed to moulder, or mercifully put down, according to the behaviour of their members and the acceptability of their chosen activity. And of course according to the popularity of their activity among the pupil population; fickleness is not the prerogative of electorates or operatic claques, and what packs them in this year can be the non-event of the decade a couple of years later.

What is needed to start them off, of course, is a group of boys (ours was a boys' grammar school) who discover a shared interest in, say, Burmese art, or Nordic mythology, or match-box tops. The second requisite is the availability of a member of staff to act as president. A better title would be *roi fainéant*, because the distinction is purely honorary. However, it is usually considered better for discipline if there is someone on the staff to carry the can when a schoolboy secretary is caught fraudulently extorting excessive subscriptions from frightened juniors, or when forty-five pounds' worth of classroom damage is caused at a society's monthly committee meeting.

Which brings me back to the unusually effusive greeting from Lewin and Traill, normally a somewhat lugubrious pair. (These were the days, by the way, when nothing so informal as Christian names was used in staff-pupil relations. This was before the Flood, you understand, when nobody had heard of tutor groups, or peer pressure, or teacher accessibility, or school counsellors, or group therapy. It was a straight case of Them and Us, with nothing to blur the traditional battle lines of the friendly undeclared war that obtained pretty universally, and which both sides thoroughly understood.)

Well, there I was, as one might say. I had to play for time till more cards were put on the table.

The best I could manage was 'Oh!'

That was enough for Lewin. It was as if I had flicked a switch, and sent him into overdrive.

'We've seen the Headmaster, sir, and he's given us the go-ahead as soon as we can find a member of staff to be president.'

'Oh!' (Not the sharpest or the most creative of repartee, I admit, but I was still groping, and what was it that Holmes said about jumping to conclusions with an imperfect grasp of the facts?)

It was more than enough to send Traill into hypergear as well.

'There are about thirty or forty of us keen on the idea, sir, and we've worked out a programme for the term – here, sir. Look. So it's not just a crazy idea of the two of us on the spur of the moment.'

'I see.'

I didn't, but I couldn't go on saying 'Oh'. And 'I see', if said with the correct inflexion, can be made to convey authority, omniscience, or imminent decision, or all three.

While Lewin plunged into his next lengthy explanation about proposed meetings and subscriptions and the election of committee members, I tried hard to think of something constructive to add to the conversation, which had been distinctly one-way traffic so far.

'Um – ' (In a schoolboy, 'um' denotes hesitation and shiftiness, and is to be condemned, or at the very least suspected; in a schoolmaster, it denotes deliberation, careful weighing of one's words, caution. . . . . *gravitas*, that's the word. *Gravitas*.)

'Um – what's this society for?' Cutting right through to the nub, you see. Direct. Decisive.

Lewin paused briefly, and peered through his spectacles. He looked as if I'd just asked him what the name of the school was. I must say he did a splendid job of smothering the scorn in his voice when he replied.

'The Railway Enthusiasts' Society, sir.'

I don't think it ever occurred to him that news of their plans and preparations had not been the sole topic of common-room conversation for the previous week.

I in turn exercised superhuman control to resist the obvious repartee – 'Ah, a Train-Spotters' Club'. Such a remark to a railway devotee would brand the speaker as a Philistine for all time. A bit like referring to Trooping the Colour, to a guardsman, as the Parade of the Tin Soldiers.

However, I had to say something, and at last something occurred to me which was, as they say, germane to the issue.

'But I don't know anything about railways.'

For the second time Lewin gave me that incredulous, spectacles look. He even pushed his head slightly forward to reassure himself that it really was a member of the staff, a supposedly intelligent man, who was uttering such inanities. He realised that he would have to spell it out for me.

'Well, it's all right, sir; you don't have to *do* anything. We run the society.'

Lewin's implication was unmistakable that I was being offered all the panoply of kingship without any of its attendant responsibilities. What reasonable creature could possibly refuse?

However, one thing that everyone knows about schoolmasters is that they are not reasonable creatures. A boy could quote, from any working day, numberless proofs of such a fact. So Lewin would be, and was, well equipped to deal with my illogical rejection of such a royal favour.

I had decided to stick to the self-deprecation line – you know, like Richard III, when he pretended that he didn't want the crown – wasn't the man for the job, didn't think he was up to it, and all that. I craftily suggested that my ignorance would be an obstacle to the future welfare of the society.

It didn't come out quite like that. What I actually said was something like, 'But why ask me? I don't know one end of a train from the other.'

A ridiculous overstatement when you come to think of it, but I hoped thereby to touch them on a sensitive spot. Would it really do for the President of the Railway Enthusiasts' Society, for all his distant pomp and dignified inactivity, to be unable to distinguish between the Flying Scotsman and a lowly diesel shunter? From my previous contributions to the conversation it was obvious that I was extremely slow on the uptake; now I had made it clear that I was abysmally ignorant as well.

As far as I could see, the only avenue I had left open to them – apart of course from a total withdrawal of the invitation – was a polite glossing over of the candidate's shortcomings and an appeal to his conceit. Something along the lines of 'well, sir, you're a jolly good master, sir, and don't you worry about the trains bit, sir, because we'll look after everything and see you're all right'.

They wouldn't mean a word of it, of course, but it was all part of the game, and I understood the rules. I was getting ready to pay for it all with a timid gesture of modesty and a 'well, if you put it like that' surrender – what the trade unions call a negotiated settlement.

I had, however, committed the cardinal error of all errors in that undeclared war I spoke about: I had underestimated the opposition. Lewin had no time for the niceties of diplomacy; life was too short. He had a problem and he needed a solution.

My final throw of the dice, if you recall, was, 'Why ask me?'

His reply had the simplicity, directness, and unanswerability of genius.

'Well, we've already asked everybody else, sir.'

Surrender was unconditional after all.

A class on his own

Nose perpetually running. (Probably no breakfast.)
Threadbare jersey – in January.
(Mother smokes her twenty a day though.)
Head down, absorbed, tongue sticking out.
(Four 'stepfathers'.)
Broken leads, errors, smudges.
'Just do your best, Malcolm.'
'Yes, sir.'
And we drone on about Culture.
How can he be so patient, so polite?

One of the posh Sundays launched a competition for the writing of what they called 'Mini-Sagas'. Each entry had to be a proper story, with characterisation and all, and it had a limit of only fifty words. My entry appears elsewhere – see 'Career Prospects'. I got as far an honourable mention, from what was apparently a total entry of about 14,000. Not bad going, I suppose – but it didn't do my career any good. (In either teaching or writing.)

This piece was a spin-off of the mini-saga idea. The title in this case took it to fifty-five words. It was conceived as fiction, but I thought it worth inclusion in a book of this nature, because it contained a very valid truth about the school where this particular child worked and the conditions in which he was forced to live.

Money for old rope

NERVES ARE A FACT of life, aren't they? The salesman hopes that the customers will buy. The actor wants the audience to like him. The comedian's worst nightmare is that they won't laugh.

By the same token, a teacher's abiding concern – at any rate when he is new to the business – is that he may not be able to keep order. Even when he has been at it for quite a long time, he can have his moments of uncertainty. Tragically, too, a teacher, after decades of successful performance, can suddenly discover that he has 'lost it'. That really is sad.

However, I once met a young chap who did not seem to suffer from any kind of nerves at all. I was only in my second year of teaching, and his *insouciance* impressed me – at first. He seemed to have the one gift I coveted more than anything else – confidence.

He certainly arrived with an impressive portfolio of qualifications, which included a B.A and a Ph.D. The story we were told was that he was filling in for a term while the authorities sought, and hopefully found, a permanent replacement. I forget what the subject was, and it doesn't matter.

If that arrangement sounds somewhat casual, I have to remind you that in the late 1950's there was an acute shortage of teachers. Practically anybody, it seemed, could get a job in a school, certainly at primary and lower secondary level. In my first school there were two eighteen-year-olds who were also 'filling in' – straight out of the sixth form. In another the dinner lady was giving guitar lessons. In my second school, I secured a post as Head of

Department, and I had been teaching only nine months. Nor did I have a teaching diploma.

This young man – let us call him Edward – had no diploma either. In fact no teaching experience whatsoever. And apparently no particular desire. He told me that he was waiting for a post to come up in his father's firm, and he had a few months to kill, so he thought he might try his hand at teaching – just to pass the time, as you might say. He had been right through the educational system – certificates, degrees, and all – so he must be qualified, he felt, to deal with the level of work demanded by a secondary modern school. This was the lowest level of the three-part division imposed by the famous Butler Education Act of 1944 – grammar schools, technical schools, and secondary modern schools (for nearly everyone else). He had watched teachers in his own upbringing, and he had peered casually through the single transparent pane of glass in the doors of classrooms, and there didn't seem to be much to it. It was going to be a doddle.

They turned him loose, perhaps a mite carefully, on some junior classes – say, up to about thirteen. At first there did not seem to be any trouble. Indeed, at the end of his first week, he confided to me in the common room, with a touch of smug surprise in his voice, 'This is money for old rope, isn't it?'

Perhaps the children were sizing him up, I don't know. They usually take the precaution of using the first few days to reach a judgment on a teacher. But once they have come to a conclusion, they rarely have to modify their verdict. In Edward's case, they clearly decided that he was a pushover, and the sky proceeded to fall in.

Before long, his class was emitting far and away the

greatest number of decibels in the whole corridor. His awards of detentions were outnumbering those imposed by the rest of the staff put together. Senior staff were continually having to go into his classroom to quell the more anarchic activities.

What had he done? Or, perhaps more to the point, what had he not done?

I cannot answer that, because I never spent any time in the room during one of his classes. But I did notice one thing about his impact on the children.

Schools have had weak teachers before, bad teachers, impractical teachers, unworldly teachers, unpunctual teachers, lazy teachers, teachers who should have had nothing to do with teaching at all. But the anarchy they generated was usually good-humoured, or at the most bored. Children who play up are doing just that – playing. There is rarely any malice – unless there are really nasty pupils there. Sadly such creatures exist, but they do not reserve their spite for a weak teacher; they are prepared to take on all comers. Often the greater the clash the better they like it.

But Edward was different. They really disliked him. It was palpable. Their attitude had an edge.

One can only speculate on what sort of verbal traffic went on between a cocky, unperceptive young man with a Ph.D. degree and a plush job waiting for him with Dad, and a roomful of likely lads who were not going to scrape up a single degree between them in a hundred years, and who didn't like being talked down to.

Late developer

You can't join in these days. On the games field, I mean. The health and safety gurus would have a fit.

They have a point – up to a point; obviously nobody wants to run the risk of a child being injured by contact with somebody much bigger, stronger, and heavier. But the gurus miss a point too. Games coaches rarely, if ever, actually join in as a full player, over an extended period. They patrol, they demonstrate, they take advantage of a situation to illustrate a truth or highlight a skill. Their participation may be only momentary. They may slow the game down, even stop it altogether in order to get across some vital truth. They can swing the whole game round in order to set up a particular situation. Like all good teachers, they make things happen, and they use the game to do it. After all, they are not there simply to referee a boys' or girls' game; they are there to teach boys and girls how to play it – and play it better. If that involves kicking a ball, swinging a racket, or wielding a stick, so be it. That is how you play those games.

You can intervene too much, of course. Nothing is worse than the coach who is continually bringing the proceedings to a standstill in order to correct a fault or hammer home a lesson. They must be allowed to play – simply get on with it – and the good coach recognises when the game is going with a swing. Even if they are not doing everything right, they are learning simply by playing. At times like that, he does indeed become a mere referee or umpire. In a sense, he is still making things happen, only this time by doing nothing.

This relationship between coach and players is not

the same as between teacher and class. A man may have spent forty minutes teaching Maths to twenty-odd boys in the morning, and then turns to teaching hockey to the same twenty-odd for an hour or more in the afternoon. But the set-up is different.

It's in the open air for a start. Fresher, often much colder or much hotter. All that space. The teacher/coach does not have the assistance of four walls to concentrate effort and attention. He often has to bellow, to give them a mental kick in the pants. This is particularly true when he is trying to teach positional play in a team game. Children are generally happy to follow a ball, but are not so good at working out what to do when the ball is nowhere near them. In that sense they are rather like a television camera at a league match. The viewer often has little general view of the whole game, and it is a rare young player who has a grasp of the situation on the whole field when he is playing.

Secondly, if the coach joins in, as he used to be able to, for any of the reasons I have suggested, there is always the risk that he will make a mistake himself, and that is always good for a laugh. Maths teachers do not make many mistakes explaining Pythagoras' theorem, but games coaches cut splendid figures if they slip while attempting a tackle, or miss a simple interception, or get their favourite off break dispatched to the long-on boundary. A good general laugh is a splendid tonic to any situation. And, if he is to benefit from it, the coach had better join in.

Then there is the obvious – the fact that lessons are lessons, and games are games. So of course the air is lighter. Even if you are working them hard, they are usually willing to put their backs into it. And they tolerate all sorts of informal techniques on the part of the coach designed to extract more effort or concentration from them. If a teacher has built a good atmosphere, they will accept no end of pushing and driving, and the coach for his part will have to accept the response that that can bring – in the shape of a good grumble, or a sharp repartee. If the atmosphere is sound, he will rarely take offence at this, because he knows that the relationship between him and them has been hammered out over several weeks or months, in mud and dust and grazes and bruises and wind and rain and disappointments and triumphs. Both sides know where the boundaries of good taste lie, and as a general rule rarely cross them.

This in its turn provokes a more lively – well, *camaraderie*, if you like. They know you are the boss, but they know too that you and they are working together to make a decent set of players.

The quips can fly.

The best way to explain, and I hope justify, the healthy atmosphere that can be generated by this philosophy and approach is to give an example.

I was out on the field one afternoon with a group of lively fourteen-year-olds, playing hockey. Some of them were highly talented, and would play for the first eleven in a few years. They were also bright.

I had just made a mess of some movement, or been slow off the mark, or simply missed the ball or something, and somebody observed darkly that my advice was perhaps not quite as valuable as they had hitherto been led to believe.

Rising to the bait, I declaimed, loudly, to the whole

field in general, in what I hoped were tones of mock censure, 'I'll have you know that I have been playing this game for over twenty years.'

Quick as a flash, back came the response, accompanied by a broad grin.

'You must have taken up the game very late in life, sir.'

Give him a big hand

IN FIFTY YEARS IN the classroom, I have been witness to a spontaneous round of applause only twice. I can not offer a reason for this. Any reader who has been to school could put forward a fair number of speculative suggestions: that I never, in all my time, did anything remarkable or prodigious remotely *worthy* of applause; that my class discipline was so fearsome that nobody dared to indulge in such an uncharacteristic break-out of emotional approval; or, to put it another way, that I was such a miserable devil that such levity was always light years away from their minds; that no group of schoolchildren would betray the cause by offering evidence that they liked anything in school that much; that – this being an English school set-up – it was simply 'not done'.

Be that as it may, it happened, as I say, only twice.

The first time came in my second year of teaching. It was my second post. At the end of the first, I had decided that I had better move to what I considered a better job, and nearer to my family roots. My plans for an alternative career had come to nothing, and I had to put my mind to doing *something* for a living. I had survived my first year's teaching with my sanity intact, if not my self-esteem. I had done one or two useful things, and I had to admit that I had enjoyed telling stories about History.

More to the point, I couldn't for the life of me think of anything else that remotely attracted me. Business, commerce, industry, public life, journalism, the Law, the Church, the Armed Forces (good God! I had just done two years' National Service). I had watched friends and acquaintances from college going off to all these occupations, with smiles and high hopes, and was beginning to wonder if I was peculiar or something.

Well, actually, there was – something that attracted me – writing. But even an unrealistic dreamer like me realised that I could not simply put up a brass plate saying 'Author', and wait for the commissions to come rolling in. A living had to be earned. For the reasons outlined above, it looked as if it would have to be teaching.

My reasons, as can be seen, were not particularly meritorious, but I had one great advantage: the country at that time was desperately short of teachers. I wrote off to a County Council in South-East England, asking for a list of their vacancies, and was rewarded, almost by return of post, with four closely-typed sheets of foolscap, printed on both sides. All I had to do was choose. Before my twenty-fifth birthday I was a head of department, and I had only started teaching just before my twenty-fourth.

I was teaching History, History, History, right through the school. Two periods a week for each class. Unfortunately, there were not quite enough classes to fill a young teacher's timetable, so the powers that be (or that were) tacked on one English class – five periods a week – 1C.

First year in secondary school, over thirty of them. And note the 'C'. They called a spade a spade in those days. 1A were the brightest; 1B were the average. Guess what 1C were.

But nobody seemed to mind. They were a cheerful lot, they were patient with me, and they taught me a great deal. In the end, we had quite a lot of fun.

Anyway, first things first: I had to get to know some names. Christian names as well as surnames. If memory serves, this was the time when the great transition was beginning – Christian names were just 'coming in'. I think too that the old secondary modern schools maintained more continuity from the primaries than did the more academic grammar schools. So Christian names came more easily, and of course the pupils were used to it. Grammar schools stuck to surnames right through the sixties – well, they did in the grammar school where I later went to work.

So they piped up, obediently, with both Christian name and surname. Till I got to the quietest boy in the room.

'What's *your* name?' I said, trying to combine businesslike briskness with friendliness as I poised my pen over the paper.

He was a stolid, well-covered boy, with rounded, slightly pendulous cheeks, a pout, and heavy-lidded eyes. Everything he did was slow; he even turned his head slowly. After an interval, back came the answer:

'Rolby.' The flattest of monotones.

'How do you spell that?'

No answer.

I asked him again. Again, no answer. It looked as if 'Rolby' was about all I was going to get. In the end, one of his old classmates from primary school chipped in.

'R – O – L – B – Y, sir. And his Christian name's John,' he added before I could open my mouth again. It was clear that he was very used to this sort of situation.

That was how I started teaching English to 1C. Not very promising. It got worse.

I had never taught English before. I don't know about other professions, but in teaching it is not enough to come at it with energy, or brains, or even a combination of the two. People who glance casually through the unfrosted pane of a classroom door are prone to jump to the conclusion that teaching is simply a matter of standing in front of a class and telling them what to do, and being three jumps ahead in the text book. If only it were that easy.

That was what I was relying on – telling the class what to do, and expecting them to get on and do it. Hell – my instructions were logical; I explained them clearly enough; I didn't mumble; what was the problem? Long before the first half-term break at the end of October, it was clear that I was getting nowhere. They were not rude or naughty; they were simply not learning – well, not enough of them were learning. John Rolby was certainly not learning. And the class noise level was well above that of your average Trappist monastery.

I don't remember the exact processes by which I tumbled to a successful method, but I do remember saying to myself, in effect, 'Berwick, you are a graduate from Cambridge University. That means you are supposed to be intelligent. Think of something.'

So I can take no credit for the aimlessness and confusion of the first five or six weeks, but I can take some for realising that it wasn't their fault; it was mine. One piece of rhetoric had been drummed into our heads, endlessly, at Officer Cadet School during National Service: 'There is no such thing as bad soldiers – only bad officers.'

Transfer the verdict; I was doing something wrong with 1C. Or, more likely, *not* doing something. Part of the trouble no doubt was that I had no teaching diploma; I had had no teacher training whatsoever. Remember what I said about the country being desperate for teachers? To get my first job, all I had done was to go and see the local chief education officer one Monday morning, and tell him I had a degree, and I started work on Tuesday – no further questions asked.

There was no in-service training in those days. If there was, I didn't get it. Dammit, there were not enough *teachers*, never mind mentors or advisers or supervisors. You just had to get on with it.

So I was on my own.

What I worked out in the end was laughably elementary. All the great truths are simple, aren't they? I bet Einstein said to himself, after he had sweated blood to sort out that business about relativity, and finally finished his jottings on the back of that envelope, 'Good Heavens! Is that all it is? $E = MC^2$?'

What did I do? Divided the class into groups, according to ability. Before I am accused of claiming that I invented the shoe-lace, I should like to point out that, blindingly obvious though it was, I had to discover it for myself, as a result of stern experience. As it took me five or six weeks to work it out, perhaps that places me pretty low down the scale, a fit teacher indeed for 1C. I don't know. But it is only when you get rid of the blame philosophy and the self-sympathy and frustration and annoyance and general misery (and only a struggling teacher knows what I mean by this) that you notice the answer staring you in the face.

Because I had been given a class called 1C, I had been teaching them *as a class*. It seemed the logical and intelligent thing to do. Remember what I said about energy and brains not being enough? I had neglected to pay my respects to the great god Common Sense. The fact that they were designated as 1C may have meant that they were all below average compared to everybody else, but it did not mean that they were all at the same level compared to each other. There were, and are, many degrees of 'below-averageness'.

Full of satisfaction about my dazzling revelation to myself, I prepared tasks of reading and writing that I judged would be within the scope of each group, and dished out the work accordingly. It involved a lot of preparation on my part, but the dividend of progress soon showed that it had been well worth it.

It worked like a charm. Did 1C blossom into rivals of 1A and 1B? No, of course not. Did the noise level come down to that of our Trappist monastery? No again. There was no educational miracle. But there was more purpose, more industry, and more contentment. They, and I, were learning something – at last.

This complicated system of adjusting work to the ability of the pupil, or group of pupils, meant that there was going to be a group on the bottom. In my case, it wasn't a group; it was a single boy – John Rolby.

He couldn't read; he couldn't write; he never spoke. Well, not to me. And I don't think he spoke much to anybody else either. His old buddies from primary school well understood the situation, and were surprisingly tolerant, even kind. There was no bullying that I noticed. He never looked miserable. He never looked anything. Every day, the same moon face, the same slow, deliberate movements, the same serious expression, the same large, rosebud lips, the same silence.

Nowadays of course he would have been speedily shunted off for a marathon of tests and various other diagnostic processes, to a succession of doctors, therapists, psychologists, child behaviourists, and other long-worded experts. But in the late 1950's there weren't any. Well, none that I ever saw. Or heard of. If they existed, they never visited our school. I never came across the word 'remedial' in an educational context till the 1970's. I did not know what was meant by terms like 'dyslexic' or 'dyspraxic'. I never heard any colleagues make reference to concepts like 'attention deficiency syndrome' or 'learning difficulties' or 'autism'.

Children like John Rolby were left to their teachers' inventiveness. They were not numerous. I taught nearly every boy in the school, and there wasn't anybody remotely like him. I had been teaching only for just over twelve months. What on earth was I going to do with him? Not only did I not know; I was completely unaware of the extent of my ignorance.

One thing in my favour was his very inertness. He was never going to be a behaviour problem. He was no threat to class discipline. He never did anything that I can recall now. But there he was, and there I was – a pupil and a teacher in a classroom. Clearly the initiative lay with me. But what?

What on earth could I get this boy to do? What could I put before him that he would recognise as within his powers? Or recognise at all.

Well – to cut out the details of the false starts – in the end, we went right back to basics – the alphabet. Yes, he did know about the alphabet (remember, he was nearly twelve). So, while the rest of the class turned to their various graded tasks, and in between supervising, correcting, and encouraging all of them, I spent what time I could with John and his alphabet. I expect some of the others worked with him too; children love helping someone who is further back than they are, and John was by common consent further back than everybody.

There came the day when I was able to announce to the class that John had something to say. That in itself was enough to secure attention. Of course, they had seen what had been going on for weeks, and they had a fair idea of what was coming. But that did not detract from the drama that followed.

This boy, remember, simply did not speak in the normal run of things. Yet we had made enough progress with him for him to be willing to stand up, in front of the class, knowing what was coming. And then....

John Rolby recited the alphabet. You could have heard a pin drop; they were all living it with him, willing him to get right through. When he did, there was a spontaneous outburst of clapping. I cannot remember at this distance of time whether John smiled, but I like to think that he did. It would have been very fitting.

I have often jokingly referred to this incident as one of my greatest educational achievements – you know, Cambridge MA and all – getting a boy to say his alphabet. But the credit belonged to John himself and the class who helped and encouraged him. In any case, I am not telling the story of educational triumphs; I am telling the story of two incidents involving applause in the classroom. All right, so the class saw it as a triumph; that was why they clapped. But the triumph was John's, not mine.

However, the second instance of classroom clapping I can take some credit for, because I engineered the circumstances which led up to it.

By coincidence it was an English class again, and it

was also a 'C' class. But 3C, not 1C. And not a secondary modern school, but a grammar school. And, being 3C, they were older, rising fourteen. About twenty-five of them. So a slightly different proposition.

By this time, I had been teaching six or seven years, and so had learned some rudiments of my trade. I had come to realise the importance of regular work, regular routines, formality, of timely but well-controlled injections of humour, of doing what you said you were going to do, of marking and returning homework promptly, and so on.

Being a C form, they were under no illusions about their scholarly expertise. They were happy to be given weekly tasks to do, and to have them properly marked and discussed in a later post-mortem session. They had no pretensions and very few hang-ups. And we bowled along contentedly.

It so happened that our blackboard was not the traditional board-and-easel design. It wasn't black, for a start; it was green. Some expert or other had recently decided that green was a much more 'restful' colour than black. So blackboards all had to be repainted. Looking back, one is tempted to wonder why they didn't paint the furniture as well. Some of our desks and benches could have done with a face-lift.

Another 'modern' feature of our 'greenboard' in 3C's classroom was that it wasn't a single board; it was constructed like a sash window, so that you could slide the front one up and down, to cover or reveal the one behind according to wishes or plans. In truth, a common enough design.

Well, my plan that morning was to do a lesson on some point of grammatical or linguistic style. Before they came into the room, I had set out, on the front board, various words and phrases and sentences to illustrate what I was going to explain. Over the previous four or five years, I had done this several times, and I knew from experience that, after I had set out the main points, there would be a round of questions about exceptions and logical problems. It would always necessitate a second round of writing on the board to settle their doubts and objections.

I expect you are ahead of me. This time, I wrote out these answers on the second board first, and masked it with the front one, with the introductory material on it.

They came in. We got to work. I explained the main points of the lesson. As I expected, the hands went up.

'But sir, how do you explain. . . . '

'That's all very well, sir, but what you going to do when. . . . '

'Haven't you forgotten something, sir? What's going to happen when. . . . '

I listened smugly to this cross-examination till they had run out of ammunition, and were sitting there, grinning with delight that they had raised enough objections to scupper 'Sir's' arguments. Then, with a one-handed flourish and without even looking at what I was doing, I flung up the front board and revealed all the answers on the back one.

That was when I got my round of applause. 'Sir's' great coup. It was a very happy moment for us all.

Us don't 'ave no books, sir

IT IS A SHOCK to a teacher to come up against a deprivation in a pupil which he had not anticipated. Common sense and basic experience have taught him to be aware of the prevalence of what one might call 'routine' difficulties – a shortage of money in the family, a lack of physical co-ordination in athletic activities, a bereavement, a divorce, an obvious diffidence, a nervous tic, a stammer, and so on. He can recognise these, and make due allowance for them.

But he can slip up in circumstances in which a particular deprivation simply had never occurred to him. And if a coming activity is likely to show up a pupil's disadvantage because of this deprivation, it is up to the teacher to devise a way round, over, or through the problem.

This was brought home to me when I was teaching English to a group of sixteen-year-olds in a country comprehensive school. They were not taking the old 'O' Level exam; they were taking CSE – the Certificate of Secondary Education. This had been devised by teachers and educationists in the non-grammar schools, who knew that the lofty atmosphere of 'O' Level was beyond the reach, even the aspiration, of a large percentage of pupils. It would be unfair to describe it as a poor substitute for 'O' Level. It wasn't anything of the kind. It was an alternative to 'O' Level, a yardstick by which pupils of non-academic ability could measure their achievement – and God knows, there were plenty of them.

Anyway, I was involved in a CSE English Language course for a group of these boys and girls. So we wrote the usual essays and did the usual exercises and had the usual post-mortems on their homework. They made progress according to their ability, their willingness, and their interest. Were they thrilled to be doing CSE English Language? I doubt it. But most of them were prepared to give it a fair crack of the whip; their self-respect moved them, for the most part, to do the best they could. They appreciated that the exam had been tailored for pupils of their ability range, so they were not subject to the sense of hopelessness which would have descended upon them if they had been forced to attempt a lofty academic height which even the slowest of them could see was beyond them at the outset.

This was the trick for the teacher to learn. These children were never going to be academic scholars, but the world needed a lot more than mere academic scholars, and it was up to the teaching profession to get them up to the highest level of which they were genuinely capable. That often meant getting them up to a higher level than they themselves thought they were capable *of*. It was often a battle against low self-esteem. This was the genesis of the whole CSE movement – to give children of below-top-level ability the confidence to consider that the effort was going to be worthwhile, because the targets were within their range.

Well, they were usually willing to have a shot at the written part. But the exam also contained an oral element. One requirement was that each candidate had to give a five-minute talk. A formal, joined-up, proper lecture, albeit lasting only five minutes.

This gave most of them the horrors. Hardly surprising; it gave some of the cleverest children the horrors. It gives a lot of adults the horrors – to stand up, face a group of people who are there specifically to listen to you, and string together some sentences in a logical manner so that you are audible, coherent, and – if possible – entertaining too. A tall order. (I have had some teaching colleagues – people whose profession it is to stand all day and every day in front of a class and talk – who will not take a school assembly.)

I had learnt from my experience in teaching games that it is no good simply throwing them in at the deep end. Yes, I know it makes a good story in a swimming context, and many a tale has been told about how somebody learnt, very quickly, to do a frantic dog-paddle to the side of the bath. But I wonder how many instances there have been of a teacher who was forced to jump in and do some speedy rescuing when the 'deep-end' technique had not worked.

I was never a swimming coach, but I was once landed with the task of introducing groups of eleven-year-olds to the business of hurdling. As with most athletic activities – bowling in cricket, flicking a ball in hockey, high-jumping, leaping over a vaulting horse, and so on – the majority of boys (I have not taught games to girls, so I don't know) will have a go, and will, after a few false starts, make a reasonable fist of it. But there are, and there always will be, those with less strength, or less co-ordination, or less courage, or less confidence, who will shy away. So how do you get *them* to do it?

The short answer is, of course, that you don't – not all of them. But you can, with some thought, some imagination, some encouragement, and some humour, induce a significant proportion of those non-benders to achieve a modicum of success.

Hurdles are not very high, but they look it to those who are terrified at the thought of what might happen if they catch their toe or their instep against the top bar as they leap at it – at speed. (There is no way you can jump over a hurdle slowly just to be on the safe side.)

So what do you do? You break it down. The process, not the hurdle.

I produced a piece of rope, say, about the thickness of a little finger. I gathered the beginners round me, carefully leaving the demonstration hurdle in the background. I laid the rope on the ground

'Now, gentlemen, for something serious. What I want you to do is run up to this rope and jump over it. It's hard, and it will demand all your concentration. Do you think you can manage it?'

Squeals of amusement all round.

'All right. Then prove it. Get in a line, run at the rope, as it lies there – on the ground – and jump over it. Off you go. Careful, now.'

More squeals of delight as they all performed the feat.

'Right. Excellent. Wonderful. Remarkable. Now it gets difficult. I want two volunteers.'

No problem there. I told them to crouch about five or six feet away from each other, and to hold an end of the rope in the palm of a hand. There must be no grip from the thumb. The rope was to be held so that the middle of it was about three inches off the ground.

'Remember, no grip. If the rope is struck, it will simply fly off the hand with no snagging.'

I turned to the group.

'Can you manage that?'

Yes, they thought they could manage that. More chuckles.

And of course they did.

You can work out the rest. A pair of boys took it in turn to hold the rope, carefully, in the palm of their hand, with no grip – three or four inches higher each time.

Of course there were bound to be a few snaggles, but it was more likely to be the result of misjudgment or lack of concentration rather than worry or fear. The reaction was general amusement that somebody had managed to make a mess of a simple procedure, which the perpetrator usually joined in with, and he often got it right next time. We had eliminated a large crowd of pit-of-stomach butterflies.

At the end of the business, I brought forward the hurdle, and, with a magician's flourish, 'proved' that they were now jumping over a rope that was *higher* than the hurdle.

Then – and only then – I got them to have a go at the hurdle itself. Was it a hundred per cent success rate? Probably not; I can't remember. But I will claim that a bigger proportion of them were willing to have a go than would have done so without that little charade with the rope.

Break it down. How was I to induce these CSE English Language candidates to sustain a five-minute lecture – even to attempt it? When those pit-of-stomach butterflies were running riot all round their insides, and, mingled with a consuming sense of total inadequacy, produced a chemical reaction of impotence, embarrassment, and futility?

As Einstein said, Relativity is quite simple. Half an hour in the presence of a boring teacher can seem like half a day; half a day in the company of a pretty girl can slip by as if it were five minutes. That's Relativity.

Well, those five minutes loomed like a prison sentence.

Break it down. First, the nerves. Talking to more than one person at a time. Without being too conspicuous. How to get them to say something that required no thought, and therefore no contemplation of failure. The rope on the ground.

So I put one of them in the teacher's chair. Low down. At the same level as the class. Not conspicuous, you see.

'Now, tell us the story of *Goldilocks and the Three Bears*.'

Blank face. Incredulity.

'That's right. *Goldilocks and the Three Bears*. You know it, don't you?'

A blank nod – if such a thing was possible.

'Well, do it. We're all dying to hear it.'

So – they do. *Sotto voce*, maybe. Mumbled, probably. Blushes and giggles, yes. But they get through it.

By the time you have got several of them to do it, the class, if you're lucky, is aware that they are sharing in a joint experiment, not being subjected one by one to a piece of psychological torture. And one is usually not short of laughs.

Then you lift the rope a few inches. Get them to do it standing up. Get them to do a different story, without warning. Get them to stand out away from the desk, with no furniture to camouflage half the body. In full view of everyone.

Bring the others into it. Ask them to chip in if they spot an error in a familiar story, a glaring omission, or whatever. And if they do, they take over the narrative.

Slowly, you are moving them on to tackling the next obstacle – fluency. Putting more than two or three sentences together, all at one go.

A bit like the BBC's *Just a Minute*. If they pause or say 'Er – ' or 'Um – ', kill them off and let the challenger take over. Have a prize if you like (though I must say I can not remember my generosity stretching that far).

I can offer no statistics about success rate. I taught scores of pupils in this course, and it was a long time ago, and I didn't keep charts of comparative progress, and if I did I can't remember what they said. But I like to think that they were slightly better at the end of it than they were at the beginning, and we certainly had some fun.

However, that did not get us over the biggest hurdle of all – the topic. What on earth were they going to talk *about*? Again, five minutes may not sound much. It never does, until you are the one who has to get up there and do it. And it has to be a lecture, not something recited from a typed script.

Again we were up against the lack of self-esteem. Young people, for all their frequent arrogance, and brashness, and certainty, and sheer noise, can often be touchingly honest and perceptive about the gaps in their knowledge and experience. Sometimes too much so. It was often a case of opening up their minds, to show them that there was a great deal more there than they had imagined. Because they knew certain things well, they often assumed that everybody else did too, and so that they would be bored by such knowledge. Not so. There was also the misconception that, because one had certain knowledge in sufficient quantity to be able to talk about it, one somehow had to be academic and bookish and clever. Again, not so.

For instance, I discovered that one girl did some work for St. John Ambulance. All she had to do was talk about what she had learned. Another boy was devoted to the scouting movement. That was easy too. All we had to do was unlock their knowledge.

But there was one boy I remember who did not seem to have any topic at his fingertips. We were getting near the deadline. He came to me and confessed that he couldn't think of anything to talk about.

He wasn't remotely academic. He was a modest performer with a pen in his hand. He was a lovely lad – polite, well turned out, attentive, quiet, with the makings of a first-class citizen. But he was one of those rare people who, if he couldn't think of anything to say, didn't say anything. Came from a farming family.

I tried all the usual suggestions – a favourite TV programme? No, they didn't watch TV much – out in the fields most of the time. A figure from history? No, he wasn't doing History. Scouting? Swimming? Riding? No time for that – the fields again. So it went on.

'Well, I said, just pick up a book in the house, look through it, find an interesting chapter, and write about that. Anything will do. It's only five minutes.'

I was checkmated again.

'Us don't 'ave no books, sir.'

This was the shock I was talking about at the beginning. Just as you take cleaning your teeth in the morning for granted, so I had taken for granted that there were a few books – just a few – in every household. I couldn't imagine a life without books. Well, it was clearly high time I started to do so.

So we talked. About his life in school, and games, and home life, and his family's farm, and what sort of work they did, and how much he helped out with his father.

And the subject of ploughing came up. More to the point, the subject of ploughing competitions.

It turned out that he did his share of helping in this too. And there it was – our topic ready made. It had been under his nose all the time.

The day came. A colleague and I had to listen, together, while the candidate gave us his five-minutes' worth. We asked whatever questions came into mind, to see how well he knew his subject, and how well he could think on his feet. And we awarded a grade.

This boy, whose family 'didn't 'ave no books', launched into an explanation and discussion of ploughing competitions that held the pair of us spellbound. It was totally removed from the experience of either of us; it was delivered with no affectation whatever; the candidate knew his subject so deeply that there was no scratching around for something to say, and certainly no sign of nerves; and when we asked questions, the answers came fluently, with his lovely accent, from what was obviously a deep reservoir (especially considering his years) of knowledge and experience. It was a pity that we had to bring him to a stop.

Incidentally, we had a similar boy who talked about his allotment. He was fascinating too.

You live and learn.

The best policy

'Those notes you are preparing on the Indian Mutiny – have them ready by Monday. I should like to see them.'

The reaction of the History section of the Lower Language Sixth was entirely predictable. Half of them made noises indicating a wide range of emotions – disapproval, injury, disgust, amazement, disbelief, and despair. The rest, less demonstrative, gave that slight raise of the head and eyebrows which signified that this unfair burden of work was yet further proof, if further proof were necessary, that their History teacher was a taskmaster so stern and callous that they would have welcomed his supersession by a Guards drill sergeant.

Well, I had been teaching just long enough not to rise to that one. One does not meet incipient mutiny with challenge; that is asking for trouble. Never attempt to crush a mutiny until they are practically tying you to the mainmast. The strategy (or the tender hope, depending on your level of self-confidence) is that, by pretending that it is not there, it will go away. This was the time-honoured method employed by our empire-building forefathers when faced with a gaggle of surly natives or muttering coolies or grumbling porters. Calculated unawareness; lofty pretence that nothing untoward is happening. One of those mutineers has got to come straight out and tell you that they are going to tie you to the mainmast.

So, as with any teacher who wishes to survive, blind eyes and deaf ears were turned, and the lesson was resumed as if nothing whatsoever had disturbed the even tenor of the well-constructed lesson.

The trouble with this method (well, in the classroom,

anyway; I can not speak with experience about empire-building) is that the stricter and the tighter the instructions you give, the more vital it is for you to see that they are carried out. You have chosen not to take up their challenge, but it is more than likely that some of them will take up yours. If you are fairly new to the business, the problem becomes that much more acute. In other words, you have to be ready when they try it on.

So, promptly on Monday morning, I was indeed ready, with every available wit collected and sharpened.

Appearances are of vital importance in these matters. The pupil, on his side, has to present his work with a finely-judged blend of nonchalance and respect: nonchalance, to indicate that the work had presented no significant problem and that what he, the pupil, was offering was no more than proof of invariable habit – work properly done, thorough, and punctual; respect, to make the teacher feel good and so swamp his natural suspicion with a flood of good humour. Quiet dignity, faultless manners, and the gentle quip had been known to secure approval for half a set of notes on the Indian Mutiny, somebody else's notes on the Indian Mutiny, or even no notes at all on the Indian Mutiny, but last month's essay on the Corn Laws with the title appropriately modified – the master being so busy or bemused by charm that any sheets of paper with handwriting on them would have passed muster. (There is the added advantage in this particular case that whereas essays might get pretty thoroughly read, *nobody* reads *notes*.)

On the other side, the teacher has to convey the impression that he knows everything, misses nothing, and that he had the rare gift of being able to take in at a glance all the contents of a written page. This illusion of Olympian omniscience can be enhanced, according to some authorities, by the frequent raising of the eyebrows or by the uttering of noises like 'Hmmm' during the course of an offhand perusal. Faced with notes purporting to be an account of the Indian Mutiny, you simply race through them looking for words like 'sepoy' and 'suttee' and 'Cawnpore' and 'relieving army'. If they appear in sufficiently large numbers, it is a fairly safe assumption that the work is not a second outing for an analysis of Chaucerian style as expressed in *The Pardoner's Tale*.

Indeed, the bluff and counter-bluff that goes on in the classroom would make the poker players of the Old West seem open-faced novices by comparison. And, in the classroom as at the poker table, you get to know, in time and by bitter experience, who your biggest bluffers are.

So I knew, that Monday morning, that a cursory glance would do for people like Walsh and Strover and Harding, but that rather more careful attention was needed to the alleged notes on the Indian Mutiny submitted by Harriman and Catchpole.

It was clear from the amount of what they had produced that it was not half a set of notes. It was equally clear, because I had taken care to become familiar with their handwriting, that it was not somebody else's notes. In fact, Harriman's piece was quite well written, but then he had brains if he cared to use them. Turning to Catchpole's work, I found that it too was unusually efficient. Again, in my pious desire to give the benefit of the doubt, I admitted to myself that Catchpole was not entirely devoid of grey matter either.

It was only when I laid the pages down beside Harriman's that two or three phrases of suspicious similarity leapt out at me from both. With the gleam of battle in the eye, I swiftly compared each version from beginning to end; they tallied exactly.

I sat back for a moment to savour the taste of victory. After all those months of listening to excuses and hard-luck stories, of extenuating circumstances, or giving benefits of doubts, of feeling you were being had but not being able to prove it – now, at last, I'd got 'em. Before the whole world (well, before the twelve members of the Language Sixth, anyway), I could confront them with irrefutable evidence, rip away their veneer of charm, prove that the teacher, like the Mounties, always got his man.

But I made one small error which in the event was to ruin the big moment: I jumped to one conclusion too many. It was evident in my only question to them.

I had decided to dispense with the refinements of a lengthy, insidious interrogation, and to stake all on the sudden, shattering stroke.

'Well? Who copied off who?' (It should have been 'whom', but I was teaching History at the time, not English, and I think the refinement would have been lost on Catchpole anyway.)

Catchpole looked at Harriman; Harriman looked at Catchpole. But there was no blush, no guilt, no shame-facedness for me to crow over. I realised afterwards that the look was simply to decide who was going to break the news to me. They were in fact enjoying the situation of the criminal, who, though captured, has the pleasure of explaining to the ignorant, baffled detective how the job had been done.

'Neither, sir – we both copied off someone else.'

Career Prospects

Our comp. got a new head.
Keen to make changes.
He 'welcomed' our suggestions. Never adopted one.
Had his own ideas – for 'maximising motivation',
'individualising discipline', 'neutralising competition',
'prioritising discrimination'.
Absolute chaos. But he never saw it like that.
He's a Director of Education now.
Good with words, you see.

Peter Rowley and the Vikings

I don't suppose Peter Rowley would ever have thought of himself as associated with Vikings, and I very much doubt whether he has thought about the incident I am about to relate from the day it happened to the present.

But I have, often, because it taught me some very useful lessons. Right out of the blue. That's often the way the best lessons come, isn't it?

We were 'doing' the Vikings. The class was a large collection of boys about twelve years old, in a secondary modern school. For those whose memories don't go back further than 'new comprehensives', I should explain that for every grammar school provided for the bright sparks who had passed the eleven-plus and so were officially labelled 'brainy', there were several more secondary modern schools for the lesser lights who hadn't. (There was a third category, the 'technical schools', who were what they sounded, and who did a good job with the pupils at their disposal – the ones in between.)

This is not the time or the place to go into the great debate about eleven-plus and comprehensives and selection and elitism and dumbing down and I don't know what. I simply want to explain the picture. Peter Rowley was an average – a very average – pupil in a large class in a secondary modern school. They were nearly all large classes in secondary modern schools.

But he was a good lad, our Peter – polite, well-mannered, neatly dressed, attentive, and keen to do his best.

As I say, we were doing the Vikings. After a few lessons and a homework or two, we knew about where they came from – all those fjords; how they travelled – the famous longships, always good for a drawing homework; their weapons, their dress, their methods, their awful anti-Christian activities; the burning, pillage, and general destruction. On a good morning, we even managed a thought or two not on *how* they did all these things, but on *why*. You need a good still, fresh morning for heavy stuff like this, preferably early in the week; their philosophical antennae are not at their sharpest on a windy Friday afternoon.

Well, we had got it across that these Vikings were quite something; twelve-year-old boys are always prepared to give an ear to anybody who can raise a bit of Cain.

Anyway, early the following week, I thought it was about time we did a spot of revision, to try and find out how much had been soaked up by the sponges of the inner ear, and how much had gone straight through and out the other side.

What do you do in revision sessions? You don't need me to tell you that. You may not all have been teachers, but you have all been pupils. You have sat through the round-the-class questions; you have read, and re-read, the relevant chapter in the text book; you have sweated over the short-answer snap test.

As a way of ringing the changes, I plumped for a map. You can't beat a good map. But it wasn't going to be me doing the map-drawing – oh no. We were going to have a bit of fun; *they* were going to do it. Wriggles of delight all round. This sure as hell beat snap tests.

I wanted a volunteer. No shortage of hands. Even when I told them that they would have to reproduce with chalk and blackboard the coastline of Norway. And the most vigorously waved hand of all belonged to Peter Rowley.

I nearly hesitated. Peter, as already explained, was not the greatest historical scholar in the class, and he was certainly not the best draughtsman either. But he had grasped one or two salient features of the Viking saga. And when the Peter Rowleys of this world grasp something, they hang on tight. If there was one thing our Peter thought he knew about, it was Norway and long coastlines – and fjords. Peter could imagine the long ships nosing out of those Arctic inlets in the medieval northern mist as plainly as if he had seen them with his own eyes.

Wondering what I had let myself, and the class, in for, I passed him the chalk as he surged out of his desk towards the board. The audience waited in a fidget of scepticism. It is not only teachers who have a shrewd idea of the abilities of the pupils in the class; it is the pupils themselves. If you ever want hard-bitten realism when it comes to assessment, ask a member of the group about the others; they don't miss much.

Well, we all got a surprise.

Peter wisely started at the top. He didn't know it was the North Cape, of course, but he knew that it made sense to start high, and work your way down.

There was no rushing; there were no sweeping flourishes, no erasures of uncertainty. Peter stuck out his tongue, and set about working his way in and out of every single fjord on the Norwegian coast. Not a single indentation was missed. At any rate, that was what it looked like.

Concentration, like yawning and laughing, is infectious. Long before he was on fjord number five, the room was totally silent. Thirty pairs of eyes were following every quiver of the chalk. In less than a hundred seconds, Peter secured with unconscious ease what every young teacher, and quite a few mature ones, strive for – total involvement with what was going on at the blackboard. Every child in the class was drawing that map with him.

Whether the map was accurate was beside the point. It was about Norway, it was about Vikings, and it was about fjords. And Peter got that message across with total memorability. Well, *I* remembered; I don't know whether the class did. Or Peter.

It taught me several very valuable lessons.

Firstly, the value of two-way traffic. Participation. Get them involved. Blindingly obvious, perhaps, but it is useful to be reminded about it nevertheless.

Secondly, children love being able to show what they can do. The more so if it is something that is usually performed by the teacher, like writing – or in this case drawing – on the board. Whether they do it well or badly doesn't matter; the important thing is that they do it. It does their ego such a power of good, and children can do with all the boosts of confidence they can get.

Thirdly, the power of concentration. You can transmit concentration, like a wireless signal. You don't have to tell them to concentrate; all you have to do is concentrate yourself, and they catch the vibes. And curiously, the more detailed and finicky the procedure is, the more the vibes will resonate.

I doubt if Peter, in the whole of his subsequent school career, ever had a class so completely with him as he did that day. If only he had known.

Kimber

Let me tell you about Kimber.

Kimber was one of those boys who, round about thirteen, started to grow out of his wrists and ankles. He shot up. And his energy shot up with it. There was suddenly so much of him, and wherever he happened to be – like a school desk – the space available for him suddenly seemed so inadequate. He was restless; he was a fidget; he was forever turning round; he couldn't bear to miss looking at whatever sound attracted his Jodrell Bank ears.

He was not a bad lad. True, not one of your great intellects. They could have drained brains like Kimber's out of England till the cows came home, and the nation's genius bank would not have been diminished by more than half a per cent. Nor did he have what one might call a thirst for knowledge. Most of his resources in a classroom were devoted to keeping his backside in some kind of proximity to the seat of his desk and his front facing forwards. Sitting still must have been agony for him.

But he was not antagonistic. He did not plan mayhem before the teacher came into the room. He was not a smart-arse who was always on the look-out for a chance to win a verbal duel with authority. He did not inject disruptive comment into the proceedings; he did not spoil sensitive moments which the teacher had laboured for half the lesson to set up; he did not spend time thinking up awkward questions.

He was a cheerful, self-deprecating, over-limbed lad who had no intellectual pretensions whatever, and who regarded school as just something you got by as you got by everything else. There was no malice in him.

So why was he such a pain?

Well, of course he wasn't a pain to anybody else; he was only a pain to a teacher. And it was because he was such a pain to a teacher that the rest of the class found him a source of entertainment; anything which made Sir go bananas must be a hoot.

So – to repeat – why was he such a pain?

Well, think for a moment of what teachers constantly demand – peace and quiet, bowed heads, the heavy breathing of total concentration on the task in hand, the scratch of twenty-five or thirty pens and pencils moving in beaverish unison, interrupted only by the rasp of a pencil-sharpener or the rustle of yet another page of the exercise book being turned over.

But teachers are not satisfied even with that; they want similar silence when equipment is being given out, books are being distributed, cupboards and drawers are being closed, and pupils are being paired off with each other. There is not a single movement in a classroom which can be done to the teacher's satisfaction if the slightest murmur intrudes. 'Quietly!' It's the only adverb they know.

To these aspirations, therefore, Kimber was total anathema. He was a walking virus to the computer programme of the lesson. Turning round involved talking, of course. Kimber was a sociable soul; he wanted to know how his mates were getting on; what they thought of the problem in front of them (like him, not much); how long they thought it would take; whether the rest of it would be set for homework; how they could get out of doing homework altogether; what was school lunch going to be today; had they noticed that Sir's shoelace was undone, and that, with any luck, he might trip over – good for a laugh any time; had they seen the latest episode of *Doctor Who*; and did they know the one about the gym mistress, the hockey stick, and the pink garter.

What about the teacher's sense of order? Surely he could control his class, couldn't he? There was such a thing as verbal correction. True. And turning wrath on to a single boy – *pour encourager les autres*? True again. Punishments, sanctions, detentions, keeping in, deprivation of privileges – was this list not enough for the most querulous of teachers?

Normally, yes. But then most classes did not contain a Kimber. You could impose the most draconian of penalties, and it would not limit his activities for more than a few minutes. After that, he would start again. It was not that he had any contempt, even disrespect, for the teacher; he probably quite liked him. I repeat, he was a sociable soul, with no malice.

He just forgot. Or rather he suddenly thought of something else that simply had to be said to the boy behind or beside or in front of him, and its urgency drove all other thoughts out of his head (there was not room for very many at the best of times).

Threats could be dire, frantic, bloodcurdling, bone-chilling, or diabolically inspired. He was impervious beyond total deafness.

I developed a theory about Kimber. I reckoned that if you went into the room with a six-gun strapped to your hip and said, 'The next boy to talk – I will shoot him,' and a boy talked – *and you shot him* – Kimber would be talking five minutes later.

What happened to him? I have no idea. Probably went into some business or other which demanded *camaraderie* and resource, and there are plenty of those. Success does not depend solely upon academic laurels in school – perhaps fortunately for the anonymous majority. Lack of academic glory would never have held back Kimber; with his hail-fellow-well-mettery, he would have made ten times what the average schoolmaster earned. And he might well have sent his son to his old school, come in on parents' evening, hobnobbed cheerily with his old teacher, and freely admitted that he had been a pain in the neck.

And the teacher would also have had to admit something: that, though it is easy to be driven right up the wall by the Kimbers of this world, it is difficult to remain really cross with them.

Our friends, the enemy

ANY PAIRS OF INDIVIDUALS or groups who are forced by circumstances to live with each other over an extended period have to develop some give and take if life is to be remotely tolerable. It might be a husband and wife; it might be next-door neighbours; it might be platoons of soldiers in opposing trenches, prisoners of war and their guards, even (we are told) terrorists and their hostages. Whatever they are, they are so close that they come to understand each other's plight so well that it can generate sympathy – nay, empathy. I once heard a primary headmaster say of his retiring secretary, 'Only ----- knows what I do, and only I know what ----- does.' Nobody outside that intimate relationship really understood what went on in it.

It is a bit like that with a teacher and his class. And that is odd because it is a room full of opposites. They are 'young'; he (or she – I shall stick to 'he' simply for convenience) is 'old' (well, he is to the class). He is dishing it out; they are on the receiving end. He, presumably, chose to be a teacher; they did not get much choice about where they have landed up. They have exams to pass; he, mostly, has passed his. He is mature; they are not. One could go on.

So there is a lot which can cause friction. But each side comes to know the other pretty well, and can become surprisingly tolerant. Teachers, of course, being older, are expected to make allowances for youth, inexperience, moods, tantrums, rebellion, 'problems' (whatever they may be), human failings like laziness, diffidence, depression, worry, and a host of others. Children, by their very lack of years, can not be expected to show similar understanding, and at times they can be merciless monsters. But there are also times when they can show a level of shrewdness and sympathy beyond their years.

A teacher can be untidy, badly groomed, disorganised, absent-minded, and smell of drink. But if he is gifted, they will not merely forgive these faults; they will ignore them, except insofar as they can cause a chuckle of reminiscence. Another can suffer from disabilities which could cause cruel laughter, but if he is devoted, hardworking, and sincere, these will not get in the way of a happy relationship.

Is this the norm? Perhaps not. Despite what the educational idealists preach about the desired classroom relationship – a happy, purposeful, tension-free, democratic partnership – the normal, natural, *actual* atmosphere in the classroom is a semi-permanent state of friendly, undeclared war. A war in which you win some, you lose some. Any young teacher who walks into his first lesson determined either that he is going to crack the whip and cow the inmates, or alternatively that he is going to inspire everyone towards an eager comradeship devoted to the cause of learning, is in for a drastic dose of disillusionment.

Nevertheless, there are moments, and I suppose it is these which, among other things, help to keep a teacher going.

I shall offer two by way of example.

The first concerns a student. All student teachers, obviously, have to spend time in actual schools, doing proper lessons, in front of real live pupils. Most schools have arrangements with local teacher training colleges by which they take in students for three weeks or half a term or a whole term or whichever period suits all parties. These students are attached to the department relevant to their subject, and that head of department – History, Geography, Biology, or whatever – organises the student's timetable (not too strenuous, naturally), supervises some of his lessons, gives him comment and advice, and liaises with the student's college supervisor, who visits the school to check up on progress.

There is usually a sort of 'final' visit by the supervisor near the end of term, on which can depend quite an important assessment of the student's progress and potential, which in turn can influence the ultimate grade which he is awarded.

One year I was allocated a presentable, if slightly diffident young man whom we shall call Pembury (I forget his Christian name). Easter term, I think it was, but that is not important. He already had a degree, and this was his post-graduate year, the fourth. If successful in both his exams and in his practicals (his spells in schools), he would be given the PGCE – the Postgraduate Certificate of Education – and he could be turned loose legally on the pupil population of the country.

In situations like this, you try, as a head of department, to strike a balance – a balance between giving him an obstacle to overcome on the one hand and not overloading him on the other. He is going to get tired, and he will have to discover how to cope with that fatigue, but he must not be crushed at the outset. After all, we want him to join the profession, not leave it at the first opportunity. He has to learn that preparation and marking take time, but you wouldn't weigh him down with a thirty-two-period-a-week timetable. He has to be made aware that classes of difficult children exist, but you wouldn't throw him to the hyenas in 4Q (or whatever class is the *bête noire* of that particular year).

So it's a compromise; you give him a well-judged mixture: a good, well-behaved class – if the school can boast such luxuries; an exam class near the top of the school (if the course is a two-year one, give him the first year, so that, if he does come unstuck, you have time to repair the damage with the class when he's gone); some average, middle-of-the-roaders (after all, that is going to be his bread and butter – most children, by definition, are average); maybe a remedial group, if it is not too big or obstreperous; and some games groups, if he is that way inclined. That should be enough to keep him off the streets.

It so happened that I had a very suitable class of fourth-formers (year 10 today – fourteen-to-fifteen-year-olds) in their first year of a two-year course leading to 'O' Level in History – GCSE now. There were not too many of them; they were nice children; they were enjoying the course; and we had a good atmosphere going. Tailor-made, I reckoned, for a student's end-of-term showpiece lesson in front of his college supervisor.

But it wasn't all going to be plain sailing. Our Mr. Pembury was, I repeat, on the quiet and diffident side, and his relations with his classes hadn't been without incident. He was scholarly, which was in his favour for the academic side of his subject, but he could have done with a little more general savvy and streetwise wisdom to cope with the gritty realists who make up the majority of classes in a comprehensive school. And any class, however angelic on the outside, could fall prey to the devil if the temptation were great enough.

That end-of-term lesson was a case in point. A student is nervous to start with. He lacks experience, and he knows it, and the class knows it, and they know the student knows it. Add to that the pressure of the test, on which, conceivably, his career could depend, and you have a recipe for temptation of the highest order. (Just imagine what 4Q – our resident hyenas – would have done with a mouth-watering situation like that.)

The day came. I explained the purpose of the morning's lesson, as opposed to the actual academic content of it. I introduced the college lecturer who was to sit, with me, at the back of the class, and we left our Mr. Pembury, at the front, to get on with it.

To his credit, he was well prepared. But the nerves were there, which was only to be expected. And things didn't go according to plan. They never do. As with actors, one of the young teacher's greatest fears is drying up. Mysteriously, all that material you had so carefully put together can evaporate like dew on a summer morning, and you can find yourself wondering what you are going to say next. Inevitably he made mistakes too – errors of fact, getting his words the wrong way round, an unfortunate turn of phrase – just like a loquacious sports commentator.

A bad class could have had a lovely time with him. Not this lot. They were quiet; they were attentive; they were obedient. But that was just the passive part. It was what they did actively that was worthy of comment.

They were, as I said, nice children. They were also intelligent, and they understood perfectly well the tenseness of the situation. They knew how important this lesson was to him. They did not laugh when he uttered a confused phrase. They politely put him right when he slipped up on a date or a fact, with no hint of cheek. And they asked him questions – questions which were not designed to trip him up, but which enabled him to retrieve a situation, make a point, or show his knowledge – *and were clearly intended to be so*. It was a remarkable performance.

After Pembury and the class had gone, the supervisor and I had a talk to assess the lesson. I have little recollection of the details of it, but I do recall very clearly one remark he made to me, which almost made any other comment superfluous.

He turned to me and said, 'They carried him, didn't they?'

The second incident concerned me, and me alone. The mistake was mine, and mine alone, and I, unlike Mr. Pembury, could not plead inexperience – just plain forgetfulness.

It was a History lesson. It usually was. A largish class of twelve-to-thirteen-year-olds. Mixed. Bright. Lively. And willing to have a go. The homework came rattling in week after week with no trouble. Great piles of it. That's the trouble, of course, with good classes. You become the victim of your own success. You get them turned on, they respond, and then they turn in reams of homework – which has to be marked by the time you see them next.

We were 'doing' the Middle Ages. Plenty of smashing subjects here to catch their imagination: Norman conquests, crusades, monks and nuns, the great merchant trade routes, castles and sieges, popes and archbishops and excommunications and murders – the list is endless. You can't miss.

They had two lessons a week, and one homework. Lesson on Monday, followed by homework that night, and the other lesson on Wednesday. So naturally you set the homework in Monday's lesson, and collected it in Wednesday's lesson.

At this time we had our teeth into a particularly meaty topic, and I could see how the coming fortnight or so was going to pan out. So, on the Wednesday, I said, 'The homework I want you to do next Monday is . . .' – whatever it was. 'I'm telling you now, so that if you wish, you can get ahead in the game and do Monday's homework in advance over the weekend. So do whatever you like.'

Fine. Not uncommon practice. Well understood. Some took advantage of it. Others preferred the eleventh-hour technique. It was up to them.

What upset the system was not them, but their teacher. I breezed in the following Monday morning, and announced that I would collect the homework. I went round the class, holding out an expectant hand for the exercise book. One or two duly handed it over. But several more said, 'I haven't done it yet, sir.'

Now, one or two feeble excuses are par for the course, and you can live with that. I knew I would get the work in due course. But, as I went up and down the rows, the same comments proliferated – 'I haven't done it, sir.'

I was dumbfounded. They had never done anything like this before. This was right out of character. There had to be a reason. It couldn't be mutiny – could it?

However, don't come the stern disciplinarian – well, not yet.

So I said something like, 'Ladies and gentlemen, this simply won't do. What is going on?'

Nobody said much. And my guess is that they were too polite to point out that I had got it wrong. I had got my days mixed up; the homework wasn't due till Wednesday. That's what I mean when I say that they can at times show more than mere courtesy; they didn't want to embarrass me.

However, that soon changed, when I began to get a bit pompous and talk about punishments for collective backsliding. It was one thing to feel for a teacher's pride and keep your mouth shut; it was quite another to cop a classroom packet for a teacher's amnesia, and not protest.

So somebody protested.

'Homework is not due till Wednesday, sir.'

I was halted in mid-oratory. Amnesia gave way to realisation, then to shame, then to guilt. I had gone on at them for something that they hadn't done, and they had taken it. And it was all my fault.

So what else could I do?

'Ladies and gentlemen, I apologise.'

There was a murmur of approval. But one girl near the front made a noise which implied, very eloquently, 'I should think so.'

I was lucky; a flash of inspiration came to me. I whirled round to her.

'Dammit, Rose, I've said I'm sorry. What do you want me to do – shoot myself?'

There was, predictably, a roar of agreement, and we all had a good laugh. It doesn't always work out as neatly as that.

Onward, Christian soldiers

Were you aware that this hymn was composed by, of all people, Arthur Sullivan? Many of us know that he wrote the Savoy comic operas – well, the music half of them anyway. William Gilbert wrote the words. They formed the greatest partnership in the history of the English theatre, and quotations and snatches of those operas are still part of our lives, over a hundred years later.

Not so many of us, perhaps, know that Sullivan also composed a vast amount of songs and theatrical music. Slightly fewer again know that, in addition, he produced a large number of sacred works. Traces of this holy thread can be detected in the tapestry of the opera scores. But I bet that fewest of all know that he wrote hymns too, of which *Onward, Christian soldiers* is the most celebrated. It is a wonderful testimony to his uncanny ability to produce music, in whatever genre, that edged its way into the very psyche of the nation, and stayed there, even if people did not make the association with his actual name. They recognise the tune, and, generally speaking, they like it, and can sing it.

We can identify *The Lost Chord*; we can 'make the punishment fit the crime'; we know how to become 'a judge, and a good judge too'; we agree that it is a fine sentiment to 'Take a Pair of Sparkling Eyes'; we sympathise with the policeman whose 'lot is not a happy one'; we respond to the 'Three Little Maids from School'; Little Buttercup's song, in its simplicity and charm and sheer singability, is pure genius. So too with *Onward, Christian Soldiers*. You would have to be a pretty miserable Puritan, or a rabid atheist, not to say a tone-deaf Philistine, not to be stirred by its optimism, its confidence, and its *camaraderie*.

This universal appeal, I put it to the court, stretches not only across the years and across the social classes, but across the age-groups. I first heard it when I was five, and it bowled me over.

My first primary school was a church school, St. Mary's. Right next door to the church. Nelson and Lady Hamilton used to worship there. It being a church school, we sang hymns. In the assembly hall. It was probably like thousands of other primary school assembly halls, but it was very special to me. The whole school was special. It was in such a perfect setting – the car-less, cul-de-sac road, with its set-back houses behind long, low fences and walls; the chestnut trees, with twigs and leaves skittering in the breeze across mellow paving-stones; the lichen-crusted church, the leaning graves, the crazy kerbs and couch grass, the overgrown paths between. It was so peaceful; it seemed so happy; it was so 'right'. I liked the classrooms; I liked the lessons; I liked playtime; I liked the rain shelter; I liked the sacred ritual of the morning register, which the teacher compiled with the diligence and attention to detail of a medieval monk copying Holy Writ. There was no danger of Berwick becoming a problem pupil; he was far too happy.

I was bewitched by the picture of St. George and the Dragon up on the long wall of the hall. (Up – you have to look *up* to everything when you are five.) No subsequent illustration of the legend, in book or gallery, has come near it for impact, lurid detail, and – once again – 'rightness'. (I wonder if it is still there.) I liked the evening hymn we sang at the end of the day.

> 'Now the day is over,
> Night is drawing nigh. . . . '

Above all I loved it when we marched – marched – out of the hall after morning assembly, while one of the teachers played a suitably military melody on the piano. *Onward, Christian Soldiers* was tailor-made for this procedure, and I lapped it up.

> 'Onward, Christian soldiers,
> Marching as to war,
> With the cross of Jesus
> Going on before. . . . '

If an army recruiting officer had shoved a contract in front of me at such a moment, I should have signed up for twenty years without a moment's hesitation. If another boy in the class had told me that he didn't like it, I would have been as incredulous as if he had told me that he didn't like custard, or sweets, or staying up late.

Thereafter it became a rare treat for several years. I might have sung it in one of the schools to which I was evacuated during the War, but I have no recollection. We certainly sang it at the grammar school I attended later. We sang a hymn every morning, so dammit – we must have sung it.

Another moment when it swam into my ken was, possibly, between half-past eight and nine o'clock on Sunday evenings. That was in the days when practically the only radio programme you could hear was the 'BBC Home Service'. Just after the War, we were assailed by the temptations of the 'BBC Light Programme', and a year later the long-haired set could retreat to the rarefied atmosphere of the 'Third Programme', where the announcers' accents were so cut-glass you could drink wine out of them.

But staple listening was the Home Service, and every Sunday evening we had 'Sunday Half-hour', thirty minutes of hymn-singing – proper hymns, hymns you actually knew, sung absolutely dead straight by full-bodied British choirs, with no way-out, ethnic accompaniments or diatonic harmonies (if that is not a contradiction in terms). Sounds a bit tame today, and one must admit that one did not exactly rush home to catch it. But, if it was on, and if you were in, you were quite content to listen; it was familiar, it was comfortable, and it made such nice sounds.

Well, of course, I used to hear *Onward, Christian Soldiers* there too.

> **'Like a mighty army,**
> **Moves the Church of God;**
> **Brothers, we are treading**
> **Where the saints have trod. . . . '**

The next time it popped up was in the cinema, of all places. Like thousands of boys growing up during and after the War, I was one of the cinema generation. I was an only child; my father was in the Army; my mother went out to work; there was no television; and there were six cinemas within a couple of miles of where I lived. So. . . .

Those were the days when Hollywood ransacked the classics, and English history, for 'great stories'. They thought they had picked a winner when they stumbled across the saga of David Livingstone. Livingstone was a 'great explorer' – in Africa – and a 'great man of God', so they could put in as much drama, jungle, and evangelical virtue as the studio sets could stand. Better still, Livingstone was bringing God and mercy to the black man, so that was good for public relations too – politically very correct, in the days before the very phrase was known. Better still again, the man who ventured into Africa and 'found' Livingstone was Henry Morton Stanley, a journalist who worked for an American newspaper (he was in fact British by birth, but you could skip over that, because he was an orphan). So the U.S.A. could get in on the act, which made it much easier than if they had done, say, the Battle of Bannockburn.

So of course I went to see *Stanley and Livingstone* (not *Livingstone and Stanley*, interestingly). Stanley went to Africa to achieve the impossible – 'find Livingstone' – and duly achieved it. During his stay with the great man, he had time to admire the man himself and his work. Hollywood being Hollywood, it came as no surprise to see a scene where Stanley woke up to the sound of Livingstone taking choir practice with his congregation – male voice harmony at its best, with perhaps just a dash of deep South hot Gospel – all in illiterate tropical Africa.

And what were they singing? Naturally – *Onward, Christian Soldiers*.

> **'Crowns and thrones may perish,**
> **Kingdoms rise and wane,**
> **But the Church of Jesus**
> **Constant will remain. . . . '**

I was bowled over once more. There was a bonus too: at the end, during the closing credits, across a montage showing how Stanley carried on Livingstone's pioneering work of exploration, the sound track soared into yet another rendering of Sullivan's great hymn:

> **'Gates of hell can never**
> **'Gainst that Church prevail;**

**We have Christ's own promise,
And that cannot fail. . . . '**

It was past ten o'clock, and the last programme of the day; if it had been an earlier one, I would have sat right through it all again. (Programmes were continuous in those days; you could sit there, if you wanted to, from opening time at about two till closing time – and the national anthem – just after ten, and nobody bothered you.)

I was to witness evidence of the impact of this hymn many years later, when I joined the teaching profession myself.

My third post was in a boys' grammar school. The whole school attended morning assembly every day. The gathering was brought to order by the Deputy Head. The Headmaster came in, mounted the short flight of steps to the stage, stood at a lectern, and announced the hymn for the day. The music master played the first couple of lines, just to remind us as it were, then began again, and the school joined in, making a fair amount of noise. One of the prefects read a passage from the Bible, there were some prayers, and the Head announced the results of recent sporting engagements, which was followed by the obligatory applause. He came down the steps with very deliberate care (fatally easy to let the concentration, and a heel, slip), left the hall in total silence, and that was that.

But Wednesdays were different.

Mac, the music master, would muster the choir to perform an anthem, or similar prestigious piece. It says a great deal for his energy, creativity, and ability to cajole such effort out of normally pretty philistine schoolboys that he was able to do this week after week. All right, so it wasn't the Huddersfield Choral, but, for teenage boys with no pretensions to special musical gifts, it was quite an achievement.

One week he did the whole of 'The Heavens are Telling' from Haydn's *Creation*, complete with soloists from the sixth form. Heaven knows how he, and they, found the rehearsal time.

But the high-spot of Mac's assembly magic involved the school orchestra as well. One day it was announced that the hymn would be *Onward, Christian Soldiers.* That alone produced a murmur of approval; everyone knows it, most people like it, and it is easy and undemanding to sing. But there was a definite buzz among the ranks of the orchestra as well. It turned out that Mac had specially written out new parts for each section, and it was obvious that they couldn't wait to get stuck in.

Each part of the gathering struck sparks off the other. Choir, orchestra, and congregation responded to the enthusiasm of the other two. Normally, one's heart sinks just a little when one sees how many verses loom ahead. But not with *Onward, Christian*. And when it came to the very last verse, we were in for a further surprise. Mac had written yet another set of parts which involved all sorts of descants, and obbligatos, and twiddly bits for the flutes, and I don't know what.

Staff at assemblies normally stood around the edges of the hall at random intervals. I happened to be right beside the orchestra, and I had a ringside 'stand', as you might say.

> **'Onward, then, ye people,**
> **Join our happy throng,**
> **Blend with ours your voices**
> **In the triumph song. . . . '**

Everyone was lifted. And not only by the music, and the volume, and the gusto. It was just as much 'lift' to see the faces of the orchestra; they were alight with pleasure. Here was a tune they knew, and one they liked. And here too was something slightly different to play *which was within their range*. (Again, all credit to Mac's musicianship.) Here was a chance to show everybody just what they could do. What an opportunity: they grabbed it by the scruff of the neck and they shook every single crotchet out of it.

For me it was St. Mary's and 'Sunday Half-hour' and *Stanley and Livingstone* and a smashing tune all rolled into one.

'Sunday Half-hour' might be a bit of a joke to many people today, probably a bore as well – certainly a non-event. Children don't sing, or know, as many hymns as they once did. Even when they do know the hymn, many of them won't sing. Religion is almost a stranger in many school assemblies. *Stanley and Livingstone* would look like a creaky, black-and-white Hollywood museum piece. Victorian religious values and strategies are out of date, and in many ways barely politically correct now. So be it; there is nothing we can do about all that. A good thing or a bad thing – who is to say?

But I know what I felt when I heard that hymn. And I know what joy I saw on the faces of those boys in a school orchestra at ten past nine on a winter weekday morning.

> **'Onward, Christian soldiers,**
> **Marching as to war,**
> **With the Cross of Jesus**
> **Going on before.'**

Invigilator's notes

IF IT IS BOREDOM you are seeking, high on the list of recommendations would come doctors' waiting rooms, bus queues, cricket, a party political broadcast, watching bowls, or studying the movement of glaciers. But my best bet is invigilation – supervising a public exam. One hour, two hours, three hours – depending. Inevitably you have to spend most of the time at the desk, because the less you disturb the atmosphere, the better it is supposed to be for the candidates. Fair enough. On the other hand, the instructions also dictate that you must go on the prowl every so often, and of course you must be on the *qui vive* for any candidate who has run into a problem or any swot who wants extra paper.

Prowling relieves the tension somewhat, though if you have forgotten to put on your rubber-soled shoes, it can be murder for the candidates, waiting for the next echoing footfall on the floorboards (most exams are placed in the hall or the gym, for obvious reasons of space). I had one colleague who always took off his shoes to patrol, and solemnly, if incongruously, navigated the avenues between the regimented lines of desks, like a copper on the beat – in his socks.

We all know that invigilators pass at least part of the time by catching up on their marking, reading a novel, or tackling the crossword, but we all know too that they are not supposed to. It's a bit like breaking the speed limit; you mustn't, but everybody does.

I came across a heartfelt alternative to these pastimes when I became a school archivist. The new job relieved me of the chore of invigilation (a happy release). Overnight

I had ceased to be a member of the 'academic' staff, and joined the ranks of 'ancillary' staff. No more marking, no more detention duty, no more lunchtime supervisions, no more pastoral care – oh, yes, it had its attractions.

Ironically, in the course of some archive work, I came across evidence of one man's recipe (I won't say for 'avoiding the boredom of invigilation' but) for getting through it. It fell out of a bunch of faded papers relating to an old member of staff – now sadly long dead. I knew that he had served the school for many years, that he was a bachelor, and was known as a 'character', almost an eccentric. One of the old guard of seasoned campaigners who had seen everything and was surprised at nothing, one who knew boys through and through. For all that, not a cynic, but most definitely a realist.

During the *longueurs* of a Maths exam for thirteen-year-olds, he doodled these remarks. Remember this was in the prehistoric past when nobody used Christian names to address or refer to boys.

Collison says he can't write on the paper because it is just like blotting paper.

Collison hasn't a ruler.

I suspect Davies of having a desire to see what Kingdon is doing.

Leach has dropped everything on the floor.

Cayley couldn't read 'quantity in pints'; he thought it was 'quantity in ants'.

Bishop is eating his pen. He is rather a noisy eater.

The door has opened itself.

There is a gym shoe on the floor.

Hoskins is about to attempt to use a slide-rule.

Barnes is playing with his slide-rule.

Butler is restless.

Hill is having a rest.

Barnes is yawning.

Ensoll is not very active; when I look at him he pretends to think hard.

After a ten-minute struggle Barnes has got his slide-rule back into its case.

Palman's desk has fallen to pieces.

Saying thank you

I WORKED IN A school for about eleven or twelve years where it was almost normal for classes – well, junior classes at any rate – to give Christmas boxes to their form master. Later, when the 'form master' was replaced by the 'tutor', the practice seemed to wilt a bit. Well, that is my perception; I can not claim that it is accurate or authoritative.

Round about the mid-to-late sixties, those who knew best began to tell us that form masters were old hat. The real way to organise the pastoral care of children was to have 'tutor groups'. And these groups were not to be from one class, or even from one age group. The first tutor groups I was given came from three – with an age range therefore from thirteen to sixteen.

The idea, I suppose, was that a much wider range of children would get to know each other better, and that could do nothing but good for their emotional development.

Well, that may be so. But I wonder how many of these reformers actually went into a school and saw it working, and watched the way children spent their leisure time. Like adults, they are creatures of habit. Like adults too, they tend to gravitate towards other people like themselves, and that means children of their own age. Because they are growing at such a rate, they are constantly changing, not only physically but emotionally.

Quite simply, in the normal run of things, a boy or girl of thirteen is not likely to have much in common with another boy or girl three years older. They are different animals.

It is difficult for a teacher to build much of a bond with such a disparate group, especially when one normally sees them only for about ten or fifteen minutes a day, if that. That was, and is, the 'tutor period'. Obviously it varies from school to school. Then there was another problem. If you have pupils from three different year groups, it is unlikely that you will be teaching all of them. I certainly did not teach all the pupils in my groups.

But a form master (or mistress) did. It is there, I put it to the court, that the real bonds are forged – working together at a subject, flogging through the verbs, wrestling with the theorems, twiddling all the knobs on the equipment, hammering out the errors in the homework, regularly, week in and week out.

That is not to say that the new 'tutors' did not work hard at their job. In my experience most of them did, and wanted to do their best for their charges. But it wasn't quite the same.

At any rate, I stick to my thesis that in the old days of form masters, Christmas boxes came up pretty regularly with the ration truck. Indeed, I had one colleague who not only informed his class of eleven-year-old new arrivals that he expected a Christmas present at the end of the term, but indicated what he thought it should be. It was outrageous of course, and it was a joke, but such was the bond he built with them in only one term that he always got it. He drove them very hard too – five periods a week of Latin – grinding verbs and adjectival agreements and word order and vocabulary. His 'Hairy Mammoth' tests became legendary. But there was never a word of complaint. Grumbling of course, plaintive paeans of woe about the hairiness of the latest mammoth, but never a proper complaint. He got away with murder. And he always got his present. Boys who left the school and attended another were known to write back to him and say that Latin in their new school was a doddle after all those mammoths.

So – what were these 'boxes'? Pretty well anything. Big cards of course. Liquor often figured prominently, as we shared the joke at their implicit suggestion that we were, outside working hours, unregenerate topers. I once received two mighty flagons of quite potent cider. A hockey team I had coached for a full season presented me with a pewter tankard – engraved too.

Sometimes they homed in on a perceived interest or habit. For many years I smoked a pipe. So I received curly pipes and pipe racks and tins of tobacco.

As the classes grew older, it is true that the presents became rather less frequent or regular. Again, the point about emotional development, I suppose. But, near the top end of the school, they could, and often did, begin again. Rather more thoughtful now. But for the same reasons; we had worked together towards a target, usually a big public examination, often for two years – a long time for a continuous project, especially for eighteen-year-olds.

It wasn't pipe racks and tins of tobacco now; it was more likely to be some kind of written testimonial, which could display quite high levels of perception and wit, to say nothing of evidence of research. I once got a dollop of all three from an 'A' Level History set, in the shape of a bottle of Teacher's whisky, accompanied by a large card, signed by the whole group, above and below the suggestion that 'History does not repeat itself, but historians often do'. They had clearly been looking around for that. I noted that, perhaps out of kindness, they said that it was historians who repeated themselves, not history teachers.

Another remark I treasured was a school report which a couple of girls had concocted for me. Here the bond was not only forged in the classroom; we had worked together on school assemblies, and I played in the school orchestra with one of them. And they both did sterling work every term or so, fitting plastic bindings on to the covers of huge batches of new text-books to prolong their life. It was a tedious, repetitive task, but I could trust them to do a solid, efficient job – and they did. All right, so I gave them something for it, but they didn't do it just for that. We simply had a good relationship, that's all.

Anyway, they presented me with my 'report'. I forget what the individual subject remarks were, but at the top they had put, naturally, 'Name: Berwick Coates'. And underneath was the entry: 'Form – Pretty good.' I thought that was neat, and I have often quoted it.

Sometimes, of course, the older ones write individual letters, and they can be very touching and gratifying indeed. And you have to be punctilious, and careful, in framing a suitable reply. You can get these letters form the most unexpected pupils too – boys or girls who had been quiet or retiring or even apparently uninterested. But no – it was all going in.

Sometimes again you have to wait ten, fifteen, twenty years or more. A chance meeting in the street with a busy parent with two kids in tow will provoke a reminiscence or a remark which recalls a favour or a piece of help you once gave and had forgotten about. I still see occasionally a boy (boy! he is now in his forties, greying, has a wife and teenage children, and drives an articulated lorry) who reminds me how grateful he was for my spelling tests. He, and I, both knew that he was no great shakes at English, and would never make a scholar. But he was willing to have a go at something if he thought it was within his range. So, whenever the class had a spelling test, I would devise a special simplified list for him to learn for his homework, and mark him according to how many he got right. He much appreciated this.

It is the spirit of the thing, on both sides, that counts.

In a secondary modern school, I was teaching English to the bottom stream of the bottom class. So they were no great shakes at writing or spelling either. As it happened, I was also their form master. So we knew each other pretty well.

I was due to leave the school at the end of the summer term. On the very last day, the form captain, without any preamble, approached my desk, and dragged what was obviously a smallish but very heavy unsealed envelope out his pocket. From the noise, it appeared to contain coins, which threatened to spill out all over the floor. Holding them in with some difficulty, he slapped the whole package on my desk and turned back to the class.

All he said was: 'Three cheers for Mr. Coates because he's leaving.'

As I said, it's the spirit of the thing, isn't it?

Incident-prone

SOME PEOPLE ARE ACCIDENT-PRONE, we are told. It may be because of rashness, lack of foresight, over-eagerness, negligence, stupidity, or just plain bad luck. We had a chap in our class at school who was like that – suffering from bad luck, I mean. If somebody sloshed a cricket ball at a crowd of spectators, he would be the one who copped it on the knee-cap. If somebody in a mad moment flung a hockey stick up in the air, and we all crouched and put our hands over our heads, it would be on his shoulders that it descended.

A colleague once did a hilarious assembly about somebody he knew, who broke his foot because, as he was walking along a corridor, minding his own business, a box fell off the wall. What sort of box? A first-aid box. Again, when he was in hospital recovering from an appendicitis operation, his friends came to see him and told him funny stories to cheer him up. He laughed so much that he burst his stitches. Some people just can't win.

There are others, though, who do not usually get hurt themselves, but they have a trick of setting off trains of events which can cause confusion around them. Even if they don't actually set them off, either consciously or unconsciously, they have a curious trick of being involved with the genesis of what happened. You might call them incident-prone.

In one first-year intake (I'm talking secondary school – nowadays it would be called Year 7 – eleven-year-olds) we had, not one of these fatal creatures, but two. And they were great buddies. Birds of a feather, I suppose.

Let us call them Swan and Edgar. They are deceptive, these children. They are not naughty; they are not rude; they are not even cheeky. They do not set out to challenge authority. In fact you would never regard them as any kind of a threat to good order and discipline – until something happens.

For a start, they are usually last – at arriving at the games field, at getting into a changing room, at coming out of it. If an item of kit is left behind, it is a fair bet that it will belong to one of them. So proceedings are delayed.

Then there are the thousand-to-one chances. If somebody clouts a ball and it goes off the field of play and underneath a nearby shed or through a small hole in the fence, or simply into the long grass, it is ten to one that they have hit it – and they are not games players as a rule; it was a rarity if they struck the ball in the meat, as you might say. But, if they did, it was just the sort of place where the ball would go.

Swan and Edgar were like that. If one plate in a pile was slippery, it would be they who picked it up, and of course dropped it. If somebody, by a fluke, got his stick caught up in the mesh of a goal net, guess whose it would be. They mislaid francs on foreign trips; they got lost in museums; they climbed on to the wrong train in mainline railway stations on school outings.

All without a trace of malice, either aforethought or instant. Things just happened when they were around. After a few months, the names 'Swan and Edgar' were enough to cause a teacher to wince in anticipatory nerves – especially games teachers.

Out of doors, you see. All those balls flying around. And in the school which they happened to attend, hockey sticks as well. In a classroom, they are there, under your eye, facing you. (Well, they were in this school – none of your pupil committees sitting at separate tables, with half the population showing nothing but a pair of shoulder-blades towards the teacher.) You have a pretty good idea of what's going on. Out on a games field, anything could happen. The teacher, naturally, has to follow the ball, just like the TV camera; he can have no idea of what may be happening on the other seventy-five per cent of the field. And in a cricket match, God knows what the batting side might be getting up to. A cross-country run was far worse – mud-strewn boys strung out over miles of wild terrain, masked by trees, brambles, bushes, bends, ponds, pot-holes, local army camps, deer, roads and vehicles (if the park is big enough, and ours was), and owners walking large dogs – off the lead.

Cross-country runs were fairly frequent occurrences, because English weather often ensured that the hockey pitches were unplayable. So there was nothing for it but to send them into the park for a cross-country run. It was never the most popular of decisions, but those with a philosophical turn of mind reasoned that at least it got them away earlier.

Swan and Edgar were as philosophical as the next first-former (Year 7 now, remember), and accepted the necessity of trotting round the park for a couple of miles or so. They knew full well that no teacher, however vigilant, could watch them all the way to ensure that they actually ran. They, and everybody else, well understood that there was ample scope for a gentle stroll (interspersed with the occasional burst of energy when a teacher loomed on the horizon), perhaps a pause for a sandwich left over from morning break, an absorbing spell building dams by a pond, or some fun knocking down conkers.

It goes without saying that Swan and Edgar were nearly always last. But after a while we got used to that. Rather like the little girl who knew that it was not all over till they heard the fat lady sing, no master in charge of a cross-country run could relax until Swan and Edgar were back in the changing-room.

Then, one winter afternoon, we had a freak sudden spell of bad light. Bad light! By three o'clock, it was practically dark. It became, naturally, very important that we got these boys in from the outback as soon as possible. Teachers were driving round the park in motor cars, and volunteer pupils were pedalling bicycles as well, all on the lookout for stray runners, and telling them to get back – fast. Most of them had the sense anyway to note the unusual conditions, and they had no desire to be out in them longer than necessary. So, in twos and threes, they came in. . . .

That's right – where were Swan and Edgar? It got to half-past three – a quarter to four – four o'clock. All our park patrols reported emptiness – not a muddy boy in sight.

This was beginning to get serious. For all our awareness of the freak capacity of Swan and Edgar to be 'involved' in something, common sense also told us that they were two typical eleven-year-old boys, out on their own, in a park, in the dark, with no navigational aids at all. There were banks, there were slopes, there were fences, brambles, ponds, walls – a dozen circumstances which Swan and Edgar could turn into a drama at the drop of a cap. To say nothing of ill-disposed adults. This was years before society became obsessed with child-abusers (I venture to guess that seventy per cent of the population then had no idea what a paedophile was), but we as teachers nevertheless knew that there were a few peculiar people out there. Indeed we had a boy murdered by one of them a few years later.

So we were, as I said, concerned. Even when the freak darkness began to lift. I don't think we had reached the stage of ringing the police, although I guess we would have had to if it had gone on much longer. And parents too.

We extended the search to the roads surrounding the park.

And we found them – in the road. Well, on the pavement of course. Over half a mile from the park. They were gazing raptly into the window of a local newsagent – still in their mud-plastered running gear, totally oblivious of the passage of time, and certainly of the search that had been going on.

They had got lost – of course. And they had finally left the park by a different gate from the one by which they had entered. One of the roads looked vaguely familiar, and they had concluded that if they wandered down it long enough, they would come to a road which they recognised as being near the games field. It just so happened that a few items in the shop window had caught their eye, and they were simply passing a few enjoyable minutes before resuming their stroll homewards.

I forget what we did with them, or to them. But I don't suppose it did much good. You might as well try to stop a schoolboy getting hungry.

We learned to live with them. But there was one

postscript – one final exploit – which deserves to be recorded.

A year or so after the park escapade, the School moved to a new playing field. It was a splendid site, right beside the river. Enough room for four cricket fields. Our chief games master – a cricketer – was in his seventh heaven. He devoted hours and hours to endless details of the ground itself, and the buildings – the pavilion and the changing rooms. He was, rightly, proud of what he had achieved.

There came the day when the group to which Swan and Edgar belonged had their first day on the new field. They were shown all the fitments and facilities. For once Swan and Edgar were in the forefront of the spectators, genuinely interested.

Our cricket master had taken particular pains to ensure that the fixtures and fittings were robust enough to withstand the attentions of the most vigorous inhabitants – in a word, were decidedly 'anti-boy'. Walls were solid brickwork. Benches were made of concrete, and so on.

The teacher gathered his first group round the door leading to the changing room and explained some of the finer points of the design and construction. The boys, as I said, were quite taken with it, especially after the Colditz-style accommodation they had had to tolerate on the old field.

Finally, the teacher came to the end of his peroration, stood back, indicated the entrance, and dramatically motioned that one of the boys should come forward formally to open the building.

Swan leapt at the opportunity. He stepped briskly up to the door, turned the handle – and it came off in his hand.

Back by four o'clock

Early in my third term at the first school where I worked – the summer term, that is – I noticed that the conversation often turned towards 'the outing'. In the classroom, in the playground, even in the common room. Common Room! It was about the size of the average miner's parlour, and had just about enough room for the staff to sit on hard chairs and gulp a cup of tea.

I should explain that this was in a northern industrial city, where facilities were a mite thin on the ground. Money was short – for everybody. To give you an idea, my first monthly salary, if memory serves, was about fifty-odd quid, and I was a teacher with a good honours degree, one of the professional classes. I know that inflation – or counter-inflation if you look backwards – accounts for a lot, but most families who sent their kids to our school did not have it easy. Streets were tight and bleak; there was a lot of terraced housing; clothes were regularly handed down in large families; many children brought sandwiches for their lunch. You didn't see solid lines of cars squeezed against the pavement wherever you went. The overall impression was one of sombreness rather than cheer.

In spite of these difficulties, I often marvelled at how some mothers turned out their children so spotlessly every morning. One lad I remember positively sparkled. He shone in the class. You couldn't say the same for everybody, of course, but then some had it harder than others.

Schools did not have it easy either. Our place had a central hall of sorts, with classrooms opening off it in traditional manner. My abiding memory is of dusty planking and dark paint. I don't think the budget allowed for much in the way of luxury. We had some kind of duplicating machine. There must have been a typewriter somewhere, but I don't remember ever using it. And I don't remember seeing anyone else using it either. End-of-term exams were written out by hand and copied by means of a process which left mauve ink all over the hands as if you had just emerged from a police fingerprint test.

There was a telephone, in the Headmaster's garret study. I don't recall one for the staff, and certainly not for the children. There was no television. There might have been a radio, but I don't remember seeing it. I certainly never got around to using it.

Blackboards were ubiquitous. And I mean blackboards. You know, with chalk and all.

Perhaps it would focus things better if I listed some of the things we take for granted in schools today, which were absent from ours in the nineteen-fifties: photocopiers, inter-active whiteboards, overhead projectors, remote controls, television sets, CD-players, DVD-players (we didn't even have a gramophone), and of course all the gadgets and gizmos of the last twenty years – mobile phones, PC's, computer games, world-wide-webs, internets, and everything that goes with them.

Books and blackboards, that's what we had. I've an idea that many children still used bare nibs and inkwells.

But it was a busy, bustly place, and children had just as much energy then as they do now, and just as much capacity for enjoying themselves with what they had. And what they had, once a year, in the middle of the summer term, was a school outing.

It was something that everybody was involved with, like Christmas. The whole school shut down, and everybody went. Well over a hundred of us, perhaps a hundred and fifty, aged from seven to nearly fifteen. For all I know, this was common practice in a host of northern industrial towns and cities, and it ranked in importance with the County Show in rural areas. If you are familiar with the television series *Upstairs, Downstairs*, you may recall the episode where the domestic staff had their annual day outing, to Southend I think it was. It might have been only half a day. At any rate somewhere within return train-trip distance from London. It was a humble, almost quaint event – with flurries of skirts, waves from train windows, ice creams and fish and chips, stockings off and paddle in the water, seaside cockle stalls and over-spilling public bars, squeal and cackle, giggle and roar – and it didn't last more than a few hours. But oh! what a marvellous time they all had.

That's what I mean by an outing. I don't mean a tour, or a foreign exchange, or an expedition, such as are enjoyed by so many schoolchildren today – aeroplanes, skis, snow-holes, water-slides, musical workshop weekends, wilderness camps, theme parks, art-gallery-appreciation gigs, rock-climbing challenges, and general eating-up-the-world. I mean an outing. You got it once a year, and it lasted only six or eight hours, and you made the most of it.

It began as soon as the coaches left the city limits and escaped from the suburban sprawl. Simple things like green fields, trees, cows, hedges, brought eager eyes and flattened noses to window-panes. There was so much to see.

After about half an hour the singing began. The latest pop songs. It was an education (yet another education for me) to notice how children who had great apparent difficulty recalling the nine times table or the dates of half a dozen history events which you had been drumming into them for weeks had no trouble whatever in belting out all the words of the top ten.

The coach driver was an old hand at this sort of thing, and knew the way to Scarborough as if it were his own back garden. Even if he hadn't, our deputy head had an encyclopaedic command of the local geography, based, it seemed, on comprehensive acquaintance with the licensed victualling trade. Whenever he gave directions to get somewhere, did it by means of pubs: 'Turn out just by *The Green Man*, then go for about half a mile till you come to *The White Horse*, then turn right, go straight on till you come to the last city pub – *The Hole in the Wall* – and take the second on the left. That brings you out on to the moor, and you turn left at the crossroads by *The Duke of York*. After that, it's easy going till you reach the fork at *The Miners' Arms*. Go left, and you come to the *Queen of Spades*, and that takes you on to Whitby. Turn right, and, just after *The Stag's Head*, you're set for Scarborough.' Something like that.

So we rolled on to the beach car park at Scarborough.

Luckily it was a fine day, if somewhat brisk, which children never seem to mind. So the entire personnel of the two bottom classes deposited their overcoats (those who possessed them) with the long-suffering Misses Markham and Webb, their teachers. I suppose they must have dumped them in the coach, and made the driver lock the door. They couldn't have carried them round Scarborough all day.

And here's another difference between schools then

and schools now. I worked in the same place as the Misses Markham and Webb for nine months – and it was a small staff – well under ten – and all that time I never found out what their Christian names were. It never even occurred to me to ask. We were all so formal.

The rest of the children – those from about nine right up to fifteen – were gathered round the coaches, while the Headmaster, the wise, seen-it-all Bill Johnson, told them the arrangements for the day. It didn't take long.

'Have a good look round to remember where you are. The coaches will be back here at a quarter to four. So I want you all here by four o'clock at the latest. Mind how you go. See you later.'

And that was that. They clattered off in threes and fours, and the staff were left, almost lonely, on the empty car park, in a matter of seconds.

That was scarcely surprising; they had all come to have a good time, and they had duly rushed off to do so. What was surprising was the absence of any further arrangements. I have no recall of conducted tours of local sights; of caravans of children and sandwich bags in line *en route* to the Punch and Judy; of well-drilled squads of twelve-year-olds on their way to a dose of culture.

Imagine – no guides, no minders, no guards, watchers, shepherds, supervisors – nothing. A health and safety guru today would shudder. We simply trusted them to be sensible, and to turn up on time, and in the right place. We also trusted the town of Scarborough not to spring any surprises in the shape of muggers, drug-peddlers, perverts, ransom-mongers, and touts for the white slave market. (And it worked; they all turned up later right on time.)

What of the staff, left all alone on that beach car park? Again, my memory of this is not sharp, but I know I found myself, as if by magic, with the rest of the men at any rate, in a nearby local hostelry. My memory *is* sharp about what happened next. By tradition the Headmaster bought the first round. It seemed to be pints for everyone. I am not a beer man, and I was the new boy, so I modestly asked if I could have half a shandy. These frothing mugs arrived, along with my apologetic little half.

The Head picked up his glass, said 'Well, cheers then', and tipped it up. I took a hesitant sip, and paused to glance round at the local décor of timber, yellowing plaster, and horse brasses. It took about five or six seconds, I should think. I was brought back from my reverie by the noise of a tankard being slapped on the bar. Three or four pint pots were empty, and the deputy head was asking what everybody wanted.

It was the speed and despatch which were so impressive. That, and the obvious impression given that this was what everyone did, every time. Yet another education for me.

As this was Scarborough, it was what one would call a bracing day. Gaberdine raincoats abounded. The long-suffering Misses Markham and Webb were not left with everybody's. I took a few photographs, and wherever I pointed my camera, there were groups of happily narrowed eyes, deep dimples, and broad grins.

They sang songs again on the way home, and tumbled out on to the pavement outside the school railings still in buoyant humour, with waistbands well upholstered with ice cream, candy floss, fish and chips, buns, gobstoppers, and Mum's sandwiches.

Think of what parents spend today on ski-ing trips,

long-distance cycling sponsored expeditions, biological research scuba-diving in Honduras, sailing in a reconstruction Viking ship to Norway, and cultural exchanges with Uganda. Those below-stairs servants had a train trip to Southend and the scenic railway. Our lot had window-gazing, frantic purchasing of cheap and quite tasteless souvenirs, beach-scrambling, candy-floss, crisps, and ice cream in Scarborough. I should think it cost each family less than a pound.

But everyone had an absolutely smashing time.

The road to Gundagai

The crows kept flyin' up, boys,
The crows kept flyin' up.
The dog he seen and whimpered, boys,
Though he was but a pup.

The lost was found, we brought him round
And took him from the place,
While the ants was swarming on the ground,
And the crows was sayin' grace.

This poem was included in an anthology of poetry for young people called *Iron, Honey, Gold*, compiled by David Holbrook, and published by the Cambridge University Press in 1961.

There was some lovely stuff in it, much of it fresher than so many of the 'worthy' poetry that used to be found in school books, supposedly 'good' for children to learn. Though there was some sound traditional fare as well.

I used it frequently when I was teaching English to second-form boys (thirteen-year-olds) in the mid-1960's. One class in particular showed a fondness for some of the pieces, and we had a lot of fun with them. They liked it especially when I put on a sort of Australian accent to read out a couple of antipodean verses. (Further proof, incidentally, if any more were needed, that children still like being read to.)

There was one boy who was always 'with' me. He was one of those blessed individuals who was somehow sent into the world with his happiness ready made. He was open and uncomplicated; he was clearly enjoying his school and his life enormously, and he had no reservations about showing it.

My recitation from the outback had obviously gone down very well with him. With everybody else too, apparently, because some time later, I announced that we were going to tackle another 'outback' piece called *The Road to Gundagai*. By this time, they knew that I usually began the procedure by reading it through myself – aloud – before we, shall we say, threw it open to the floor of the house.

The class settled expectantly. It is a lovely noise when you hear a group preparing themselves for what they know is going to be a pleasurable experience.

The cynics might argue that boys are capable of kidding a teacher that they think something is wonderful when in fact they are simply laying on a few minutes' laziness for themselves. True, they are – capable, I mean. But any teacher who has done a few years in the galleys of junior English (or junior anything) has learnt the difference; you know when they're putting you up to something and when they mean it. They can't manufacture that rustle and stir; that is the giveaway.

The argument was clinched by this boy – Guy Waller was his name – settling his chin on his hands and saying, 'Go on, sir – do your Australian accent.'

This, to be sure, was no great incident. What then makes it special?

Because I taught Guy the following year, and three years later again in the Sixth Form. I coached him in cricket and hockey teams. He was still the same transparent lad, doing his honest best and thoroughly enjoying everything the school had to offer.

When I left the staff and took another job two hundred

miles away in Devon, he and a few classmates took the trouble to come all the way down to visit me – twice.

Later still, after he had entered the Regular Army and received his commission, he came down again, this time with a girl friend, Susan. Then he brought her as his fiancée. Again, as his wife. There was a spell when (he was a captain now) they took a house in Exeter, and we exchanged visits. They were an ideally matched couple. He was as happy as ever. Never more so than when he told me that Susan was expecting a baby. It was a daughter – Ruth.

One day, I had an unexpected phone call from Guy's father. It was to tell me that Guy had been killed in an accident with an armoured vehicle. . . .

A few years later I met Susan again, and Guy's mother and father, and Ruth. The likeness to her father was arresting. I was amazed, and touched, to see how well they had coped – together – with this terrible disaster.

I have maintained contact, albeit fitfully. Ruth entered the same school as her father – where I had taught him. (It had become co-ed by that time.) She did well, went into medicine (her mother is a nurse and midwife), and qualified as a doctor. She is now a pathologist. It will be interesting to see how well she combines this demanding work with being married and raising a family.

Throughout all that time, the family remained welded together. Guy's mother, a most elegant lady, sadly died of cancer a few years ago, and his father died only recently.

The years respect no-one.

As I write, Guy himself would have been over sixty, had he lived. That of course is irrelevant. One can think of a person only by leave of what one actually experienced of him. I saw him as a grown young man, a professional soldier, a husband, a father, and a friend. But all that time, he was the same at heart as when I had first met him – a blithe, happy second-former.

That was the essence of him, the abiding memory – leaning his chin on his hands, grinning with pleasure, and murmuring from the back of the class, 'Go on, sir – do your Australian accent.'

Visiting a tree

THERE IS A SCHOOL in the West Country which is famous for its cross-country runs. Well, for *a* cross-country run, to be precise. It lies in the midst of fields just adjacent to Exmoor. When it was founded, in the middle of the nineteenth century, there were no cars, obviously, and no trains. The local 'bus' was a horse-drawn cart. So nobody, either the pupils or the staff, got about much.

Keeping a schoolful of boys occupied out of lesson hours was a constant headache, so it was hardly surprising that the school authorities fell back on what they had – plenty of fresh air, and plenty of wide open moorland. Let them work off surplus energy on cross-country runs. These runs became such a fixture in the extra-curricular timetable that they all acquired names – the *Tuck*, the *Bray*, the *Crossbury*, the *Long*, the *Short*, the *Stoodleigh*, the *North-West*, the *Leary*, the *Filleigh*, and so on. They varied in length and difficulty, and they all worked up to the toughest of them all – the *Exmoor*. This was the climax of the running season, and it took place at the end of March or the beginning of April.

It had been the first to be instituted, in 1859, and it is the school's oldest tradition. What is more, it was compulsory; every boy had to run it. And it's nine miles long. That is not all; they have to walk from the school to the starting point up on the top of the Moor – another six miles. I have spoken to an old boy who remembers having to do it when he was only ten years old.

The unexpected thing is that the boys (and now the girls – the school has been co-ed for over twenty years) are very proud of it. And the girls do it too. Over the years the other runs have been discontinued, largely for two reasons: one, the pressure of competition from other sports and pastimes which have grown up and which bid to fill up a lot more of a pupil's leisure time; and two, the construction of a main road which cut across the course of many of these runs. So it is now just the *Exmoor*.

The whole school shuts down for it. Early in the morning, the senior boys begin the six-mile walk to the start. Later the members of Year 7, the 11-12 year-olds (suitably hooded and anorakked, and well provisioned with fodder), are taken out and parked in twos and threes to mark the course. After an early lunch, the senior girls, junior boys, and junior girls are coached off to their own respective starting points. So in effect there is not one *Exmoor*, but four – the four courses are now tailored according to age and sex, but the senior boys still do the full fifteen miles, six out and nine back. Every member of staff is dragooned to be a driver, marshal, contact point, steward, whipper-in, medicine man, helper over gates, and search party, and the headmaster, also suitably attired in clumpy boots and multi-coloured jumper, waves a handkerchief to start the race.

It is quite a day.

The weather and the local geography regularly add their twopennyworth to the proceedings, and no *Exmoor* would be complete without sheep, hedges, ditches, gorse, misleading signposts, barbed wire, mud slides, river crossings, and horizontal rain.

Certain features of the course have not only gone into school folklore, but have been re-christened. There is a village called Charles nearby, and the low-lying land marked on the Ordnance Survey map as 'Charles Bottom' is referred to, naturally, as 'Charley's Arse'.

Put all this together – wind, rain, fog, water, cow pats (known in school formal jargon as 'bovine residue'), waiting hours (if you're a marker) for the runners to appear, getting plastered with mud from head to foot, feeling like death ('it's the Cleave that crucifies you'), taking wrong turnings, getting lost, being late, mishaps among the staff – and you have plenty of material for tall stories.

One favourite, which, despite its outrageousness, refuses to go away, concerns a chicken.

The parties which do the marking of the course, understandably, have a long time to sit around till the runners get to them. They are prepared, of course, for bad weather. They are largely prepared too for the pangs of hunger and thirst. Some wise owls have also taken the trouble to bring with them the means of cooking a hot meal. What with that, and a small tent or groundsheet, and a bottle of what you fancy, and maybe a supply of fags, it can become quite an expedition. Not all the markers in the old days were eleven-year-olds; from what I have heard, many were seasoned campaigners of fourteen or fifteen.

Anyway, this story claims that one of them – David, shall we say – decided that what would really make the day would be fresh meat. Sausages were becoming old hat. So – again according to the story – David and his accomplices repaired to the nearest moorland farm, broke into a poultry-run on the edge of the property, stole a chicken, smuggled it out, and took it back to base camp. There they wrung its neck, plucked it, and roasted it over their fire. The legend of the Phantom Chicken Stranglers of Exmoor was born.

I know little of David's subsequent career at the school,

though what evidence I have been able to gather indicates that he had been no angel before the chicken incident, and did not noticeably raise his Celestial Factor afterwards.

The next episode that became known to the school was tragic. David had gone to live in the United States, where he married. The marriage was not successful. Not long after the break-up, David was murdered. The police, it appears, did not over-exert themselves to bring the murderer of a random Englishman to justice, and nobody was ever charged with the crime. Indeed, when his distraught parents went to America to recover his body, the police let them attend a funeral service in the belief that there was a body in the coffin, before informing them that there wasn't. It had already been cremated. So his poor mother and father had to cope with a ghastly scenario of loose ends – no body, no solution to the crime, and no punishment of the criminal.

It was only thanks to the determined intervention of a good friend (who clearly knew the ropes) that the ashes were recovered. Mother and Father were allowed to bring them back to England. On a bright May morning they took them to David's favourite boyhood holiday location, Cape Cornwall near Land's End, and scattered them over the Atlantic.

Now here comes the remarkable part.

Some years later they renewed contact with the school, and presented a prize to be awarded in David's name for a particular success in the *Exmoor*. The prize involved a complicated calculation of places and points, which is not relevant here. What is relevant is that this noble couple, anxious to create some kind of memorial for their son, chose to become part of the *Exmoor* tradition.

Not only that; they came to the school every year on *Exmoor* day to present the prize, and it's a long way from Derbyshire to Devon. They were regular visitors to the office of the school registrar, Mrs. Lorraine Millar, who received them and made a fuss of them. She always made time, in a day invariably crowded with visitors, incidents, surprises, and crises, not to mention mere work, to talk to them.

It was touching to see how well they had coped with this terrible shock. Luckily, they had two daughters, and grandchildren, so they had much love to sustain them.

This went on for several years. Then father's health began to fade. He developed Alzheimer's. For a year or two he struggled to come, but in the end it was too much for him, and he had to go into residential care.

Mother continued to keep contact, by telephone. Lorraine was a patient and sympathetic listener, and they struck up a friendship. Sadly, now, mother had not only her son's story to talk about, but her husband's decline as well. Last year he died.

But she did come once more. This time not to the *Exmoor* event, but to the grand opening of a brand-new, very posh, Art and Drama block. Once again, Lorraine looked after her. She tells me that they are now in regular, if not frequent, touch by phone.

Not long ago, as part of the celebrations of the school's 150th birthday, a lot of trees (well, saplings, of course) were planted up on the edge of the campus. Pupils, parents, old members, and anybody connected with the school, were invited to buy a tree, which would be planted in their name, in the cause of the environment.

David's mother asked if she could buy one for him. Lorraine offered her services in the actual planting of it.

Would she like Lorraine to do this for her? Yes, she would, very much. So, when the Great Planting Weekend came, Lorraine put on her wellies, took up her trowel and spade, and did the business. She had specially arranged with the teacher in charge of the proceedings that the tree – a young oak – would be planted in the middle of a small clearing. An appropriate metal plaque was added.

Mother rings up every so often, and she and Lorraine have a chat about this and that. She does not ask about the tree, even though, obviously, she must want to. Lorraine thinks it is because she is afraid that it would put pressure on her (Lorraine) to make a special trip up to the tree to see.

So guess what: Lorraine, being the kind lady she is, makes a point now and then of going up to the plantation to have a look, so that she can make a report about it. She tries to choose a bright day, because, she says, if she approaches the clearing from the right angle and at the right time, a beam of sunlight plays straight on to the metal of the name plaque and lights it up.

David's Mum is very happy when Lorraine tells her about that.

Second time around

In 1858, a system for testing the progress and achievement of secondary pupils was set up all over England. That did not mean that there *were* secondary schools all over England, but the system for testing them was now there, and would therefore accommodate such new secondary schools as would be set up in the coming decades.

The universities of Oxford and Cambridge each agreed to be responsible for the syllabuses, the examination papers, the administration of the exams themselves, and the assessment of pupils' output. Examination centres were set up in cities all over the kingdom. The Oxford and Cambridge Local Examinations entered the academic bloodstream of English education.

They were successful too, and were extended to numerous countries all over the British Empire. The 'Locals', as they became known, lasted from 1858 till they were superseded in 1918. Sixty years – not bad going.

Their successors, School Certificate and Higher School Certificate, lasted until 1951 – a run of only thirty-three years. Their successors in turn, 'O' Level and 'A' Level, ran till 1988 – thirty-seven years, just a mite longer. Now we have GCSE, which has so far notched up, at the time of writing, thirty ('A' Level has survived from the previous era). With our experience of how quickly these days educational ideas, philosophies, and fashions can mutate (if you take more than a few years to make up your mind about which is best, heresies and gospels can become almost interchangeable), one can be forgiven for wondering how long the present arrangement will continue, before somebody gets a knighthood for writing a book to tell us that everything we have been doing up to now is wrong.

However, I just wanted to set the scene, to paint in a spot of background. I am concerned in this chapter with the 'O' and 'A' Level part of it – to give it the full name, the General Certificate of Education. More precisely the 'O' half.

The faceless organisers of 'O' Level had sensibly recognised that not everybody is at his or her best on any given summer's day, and can therefore not always perform to his or her expectations, or to the teacher's. So they could have a second shot in November or December.

The grammar school where I worked at the time – in the 1960's – took this a stage further (and many other schools did too); they made provision for those who wished to go right through the whole fifth year again, in as many subjects as they wished. This was in order either to improve their previous grades, or, if they had failed, simply to pass with whatever grade was being offered – and big sighs of relief all round. I remember we had one boy who did so many re-takes, in both June and December, that we felt like giving him a season ticket to the examination room.

Anyway, it fell to me to be put in charge of those boys who wished to have a second shot at English – both Language and Literature. A full re-take, the whole year. For once, the school authorities showed a modicum of sensitivity towards the feelings of a class of sixteen-year-olds who had – well, who had failed, by refraining from calling them a 'Second-Shot Fifth Form' or the 'Repeat Fifth'. They dubbed them the 'General Sixth', thus generously awarding them the dignity of other pupils of the same age, and avoiding at the same time any mention of their 'repeat' status. Quite neat, I thought. Everybody knew what they really were, but it just looked better, and sounded better. It had the same effect that Churchill wrought by renaming the 'Local Defence Volunteers' as the 'Home Guard'.

Average numbers were about fifteen or sixteen, and we were allocated five periods a week – once a day. Do a simple sum: a period lasted forty minutes; five periods a week; about 35 operative weeks in an academic year (once you have knocked out holidays, end-of-term junketings, and time off for the actual exams themselves); and you get a total of about 7,000 minutes. Not very much, put like that.

What did we have to do during those 7,000 minutes? Rather more than you may think. Take the 'Literature' part first. There were three set books – a Shakespeare play, a hefty chunk of Chaucer, and a modern novel or play or piece of non-fiction.

I took the General Sixth for five years, so this was how it panned out.

Take the Shakespeare. The *Merchant of Venice* was pretty straightforward, and the main character was at least part of general knowledge, and there were some funny bits. *Henry V*, thanks to Laurence Olivier and his famous film, got us off to a good start. But the other three – *Henry IV* (Part I, if I remember correctly), *Richard II*, and *Richard III* are not easy plays. Not a great deal of what you might call light relief.

Chaucer had the light relief (quite a lot actually, if you could work out what it meant), but the obvious problem was that it was practically a foreign language. So the jokes had to be translated before they could be explained, which tends to impair the humour somewhat. They had none of the immediacy of Tommy Cooper's 'A man-goes-into-a-pub' technique. They were heavy going. The examiners rang the changes here between *The Prologue*, *The Pardoner's Tale*, and *The Nun's Priest's Tale*.

The modern stuff could be anything. The five books I, and they, were saddled with were *The Shetland Bus* (an account of wartime derring-do in the North Sea); Churchill's *My Early Life* (which was at least full of action, and not without humour, particularly his accounts of his doom-laden schooling); two short novels by Joseph Conrad (his over-rich English was a mite indigestible to teenagers, or indeed to their teacher); and finally Shaw's *St. Joan* (with its interminable pages of preface, full of the Irish bard's blarney, windbaggery, and mischievous observation, not to say conceit – I remember his saying that his play contained everything that anybody needed to know about Joan of Arc).

And take a look at his preface. The subtitles alone are enough to put off any teenage student who does not have his eyes set on a fellowship at Trinity. Try these: The Stage Limits of Historical Presentation; Modern Distortions of Joan's History; Joan as Theocrat; Joan a Galtonic Visualizer; The Mere Iconography does not Matter; the Evolutionary Appetite. There are plenty more. The most willing reader feels about two inches high long before he gets to the opening of Act One.

That was just the Literature. Now get a load of the 'Language' half of it. When I come to describe some of these components, I shall feel a little as if I am describing a syllabus of a medieval knight's equipment as a prerequisite to entry to military college to a candidate who is trying to get into Sandhurst today.

There was an essay, of course. Well, no trouble there. Our most radical reformers concede that it might be a good idea if candidates can express themselves clearly in their native language, on paper. (Though, with the onward creep of digital intercourse, the 'paper' part might be called in question.)

Candidates then had to summarise a given passage – the famous 'Precis'. Still a useful skill. Teaches them to think clearly. One of the best questions I ever set in a mid-school History paper was: 'Explain in about 100-150 words what you understand by the phrase "Industrial Revolution".' I got some very good answers, and all sorts of others too. It didn't half sort them out.

Another passage was set, on which candidates were asked questions designed to test their 'Comprehension', as they used to say. I don't know what the regulations are today. But I dare to suggest that in 'O' Level another useful skill was being tested.

Now we move into more turbulent waters. How do modern candidates today (or their teachers) feel about Figures of Speech? Never mind the obvious similes and metaphors and alliterations, even onomatopeia; how about hyperbole, personification, oxymoron, bathos, euphemism, paradox, and the stygian depths of metonymy, litotes, and synecdoche? Well, we did those – some of them, anyway.

Indirect Questions and Indirect Speech? Verbal agreement? Floating Participles? To say nothing of commas, semi-colons, colons, hyphens, dashes – all with a set of, if not rules, certainly recommendations and 'good practice' suggestions. Ring a bell today? They did then.

And then, and then, my children, we come to the

greenhouse of good composition, the laboratory of clear sentence-construction, the bedrock of effective prose composition and clear writing – 'Clause Analysis'. What is each word, each phrase, each clause doing in that sentence? How does each part of it relate to the others? How could the mere transposition of a phrase or clause markedly improve the clarity of the sentence?

I have to tell you that a significant part of the examination in English Language consisted of a long sentence, which the candidate was invited to 'analyse' – that is, divide into its component parts. He was then asked to comment on the functions of those parts.

A candidate therefore had to be familiar with terms like Complement, Apposition, Finite Verb, Present Participle, Gerund, and Parentheses. He was required to know the difference between a Simple Sentence and a Complex Sentence. He had to know what constituted a phrase and what constituted a clause. He had to be able to recognise Noun Clauses and Phrases, Adjectival Clauses and Phrases, and Adverbial Clauses and Phrases. Not content with that, the examiners were wont to ask the candidate to distinguish between, say, a Noun Clause Subject and a Noun Clause Object; or between an Adverbial Clause of Time and an Adverbial Clause of Purpose, to say nothing of those of Condition, Concession, and Result.

Did all this make the candidates better writers of English? One would hope so. It certainly helped them to recognise *bad* English when they saw it, which is a start.

Does it therefore have validity now? Again, one would like to think so. But of course fashions change, and educational ideas change, and nobody now takes Clause Analysis seriously. They wouldn't even give it capital letters, never mind the time of day. Nevertheless, I offer this thought before retreating from the front line: nobody would trust a doctor who had not studied anatomy during his training; nobody would have much confidence in an AA man who did not know how an internal combustion engine worked. Yet young people today are expected, by some rare blend of linguistic alchemy and osmosis mysteriously absorbed in the classroom where the very word 'grammar' has almost disappeared, to become fluent in English composition, when they have little or no idea of the components of a sentence, or of what makes good style, or of the difference between the spoken and the written language. Curious.

However, I am not on the soap-box to advocate what ought to happen; I am trying to give the flavour of what actually did happen all those years ago, for better or worse. These second-time-arounders had to cope with all that I have described, and they had 7,000 minutes in which to do it.

What did they have to equip them for these 7,000 minutes? They were not particularly academic, for a start. Of course not. By definition. They had already failed once, some by a yawning margin – grade 9, out of 9. They were capable of putting at the top of a test paper the title 'English Langage' or 'English Langauge' or 'English Laungage' or (my favourite) 'English Langague'. One of them coined an immortal rendering of a house of ill fame – a 'bothel'. (Think about it; given time, it can conjure up a whole world of images.) Another struggled for several versions with the word 'illegitimate', and finally, in disgust, crossed them all out and wrote 'bastards'. He could spell that all right.

There was a physical difficulty. Many of them were great beefy lads, more at home on the sports field. Half of them could barely fit into the Tudor desks that they had to tolerate.

However, they had some advantages too. They were sharp enough to understand their limitations. It made them charmingly realistic; they had none of the dreamy aspirations of the bright sparks who had just amassed eight grades 'A' the previous summer. Indeed, one of them once confided to me in a thoughtful moment, 'You know what, sir? I shall never be cultured.' He didn't say it with bitterness, or with tearful regret. It was, so far as he was concerned, a simple statement of fact. Rather like the humble member of the third eleven who knew he would never play for England, no matter how much he may have wanted to.

From a teacher's point of view, they were easy to understand. They were not temperamental. Their realism made them more mature than their egghead contemporaries. They were shrewd. They were quick to spot insincerity, flannel, lack of purpose, and above all talking down, and a teacher had to keep his weapons of gumption well honed and handy. They had a vigorous sense of humour, and kept it regularly exercised.

A teacher had to prepare his strategy with care, and to get it across to them as soon as possible. There was a job to be done. He, the teacher, was not responsible for it, any more than they were. They were not in the business of Culture; they were in the business of passing an exam – two actually. They were stuck with it; so was he; they were stuck with each other. The only way to survive was to identify the job, and get on and do it. In short, as always, there was no substitute for work. Nobody expected them to set the Thames on fire, but, equally, they owed it to themselves to do the best they could. After all, nobody was imprisoning them there; they had chosen to do it. As always, too, a teacher had to lead. If he led, with a pat on the back here and a kick in the pants there; with a nudge on the one hand and a joke on the other, they would follow.

And they did.

For five years – five General Sixths, that is. We had a lot of fun. I read out some of their worst test howlers and essay gaffes, and everybody had a good laugh, even the perpetrators. We ploughed right through the Chaucer, translating and explaining, with a spot of levity extracted from Chaucerian vocabulary and pronunciation. 'He sholde holde his pees' – that sort of thing. Everyone had a good snigger about that.

We doggedly read the Shakespeare play round the class – right through. We shared the embarrassment of the boy reading the part of Richard III (Gloucester), who lost his concentration, and, when he woke up, found that his first line was, 'My noble lords and cousins all, good morrow. I have been long a sleeper.'

Then there was the lesson – English Language this time – when we were learning how to make verbs ending in '-fy' to indicate various processes. You know – 'what do you do when you make somebody frightened'? – 'terrify'. 'Change something' – 'modify'. And so on. Round about half-way through this exercise, a particularly large boy (let us call him Ransome) switched off and gazed out of the window (alas, a fairly common occurrence in tedious grammar sessions). We got to the question about 'what is the verb to indicate making something fertile and fruitful?' The boy who had to work this out made very heavy weather of it, despite several promptings from 'Sir'. It became obvious that the answer was not forthcoming. So, in some impatience, I said, in a louder voice than usual, 'Fructify!' Now think where the stress falls.

Ransome nearly fell off his chair with the shock of what he thought he had heard.

It helped if you whipped out a neat repartee now and again. I was handing back some essays, and had paused to indicate some errors in one boy's work. He looked at me stonily for a while, and then said, 'Well, if you must know, sir, I didn't think much of the essay titles.' A slight intake of breath all round. The muse fortunately was with me, and I replied, 'If it comes to that, I didn't think much of your essay, but we're not going to get very far by being rude to each other, are we?' The situation was defused instantly. If you were lucky enough to hit it right, they recognised, and respected, a fair cop.

They respected, too, a certain grinding efficiency. In the Shakespeare particularly, which was nearer to their experience than distant Chaucer, the thorough reading round the class, and the regular tests of their knowledge of where a passage came from, did give them a certain command. They didn't become the Old Vic, or experts on the Bard's style, but they did know the text by the time we had finished.

Proof of this came once on the very day of the English Literature exam. (*Henry V* this time.) I opened the doors of the exam room, went outside, and invited them to come in. As they passed me, one of them commented to nobody in particular, 'O, for a muse of fire!'

How well did they perform? I can't remember. I don't suppose they broke any records. But the journey can often be as satisfying as the arrival, the effort as much as the prize. I do remember though, and value, the remark a boy made to me at the end of one year's work: 'We enjoyed it like hell, sir.'

But, to keep it in perspective, and to show that compliments do not necessarily reflect the whole truth, perhaps the following might show better the essence of the General Sixth.

I think it was some Clause Analysis. Perhaps I should have said 'some more Clause Analysis'. I shall invent two more names, for obvious reasons. Down in front of me, in the right corner, sat Edgeworth, an even beefier boy than usual, heavy-browed, a mite deliberate, and a hesitant responder. In the next column of desks, to the left, and parallel with Edgeworth, rested Hoseley. Hoseley was also quiet, not, as with Edgeworth, because of slowness, but because of weary patience. He had that crushed air which shows the owner to be one who never expected much from the world, and who had a grittingly honest view of his surroundings. If you ever saw the wonderful Hollywood supporting actress Thelma Ritter, you will know what I mean – the quintessential put-upon bucket-and-mop philosopher. When, like Thelma Ritter, Hoseley did say things about life or work, they were usually brief, deadpan, to the point, and lethally accurate.

I was going round the class, firing questions about the current exercise, and extracting the usual answers; it was routine stuff. I had gone right round, starting on my left – up a row and down the next, till I got to Hoseley. He, having delivered his share of the answers, shut down. I went back up the row behind him, and down again, the last on my right, till I got to Edgeworth at the front.

As it was the last question in the series, slightly mischievously, I asked him one that often trapped them. There was an obvious answer, and there was the correct answer. After I had put the question, there was a pause, as Edgeworth went through his usual impression of deep thought.

At last, he came out with a response. It was the right one. I raised several eyebrows and inclined my head in mock deference.

'Well done! Very well done!'

Edgeworth looked blank. For the life of him, he couldn't see what he had said that was so significant.

Hoseley lifted his head and turned to him.

' 'E thinks you're dim.'

Could do better

As I sit down to write this, I have in front of me a school report written on a boy over ninety years ago. To be precise, for 'the term ending December 14th, 1921'. Apart from his name, his age, class, house, form order – and of course the printed names of the subjects – the entire report – that is, what his teachers actually wrote about him – consists of twenty words. Five subjects, twenty words. The word 'good' appears twice, the words 'progress' appears twice, the word 'very' appears twice, and the word 'satisfactory' appears three times. The only spark of individualism came from a teacher who was moved to write 'keen, intelligent & successful'.

On the basis of this information, the Headmaster wrote 'an excellent report in all ways'. Make of that what you will.

Is it simple testimony to the fact the teachers are a lazy bunch of automatic pilots? Is it evidence of the 1920's, public school, Bulldog Drummond gift for stiff upper-lippery, understatement, and avoidance of any suspect emotion or enthusiasm? (Harking back to 'going over the top', or Captain Oates telling his companions that he was 'just going outside and may be some time'?) Or, on the contrary, does it reveal that the teachers are in fact very realistic, and know that such bland statements are usually all that is required; the boy is bowling along pretty well – as most boys do – and there have been no dramas or causes for worry? If there had been, no doubt father would have been on the receiving end of an individual letter from the Headmaster direct, inviting him to come in and have a chat.

It is certainly the view of most children. They just get on with things, and are not given to analysis. Think of the question that mother and father put so often to their offspring: 'How was school today?' 'Oh, all right.' That's about all you get. That's about all they think is necessary.

Or again, does it reveal even greater depths of realism, verging on the cynical? Most teachers know that parents rarely read more than a small percentage of the documents that the school sends to them. Witness the number of telephone enquiries the school secretaries receive about the date of the start of the new term, or the excuses sent to the teacher in charge of a school trip, saying that they did not know that the full balance of costs was due the previous week.

Let the cynicism spread further. Was the Headmaster under severe pressure that particular term, and had his subject teachers had been very tardy with the submission of reports? So did he cut a corner by writing some of his reports first and *then* circulating them to his colleagues? Rather like Edgar Wallace, who famously got the sack from his editor for writing a detailed report of the arrival in Liverpool of a transatlantic liner which had never set sail from New York.

Then again, was it a case of the Headmaster wanting all his geese to be swans? If too many of his pupils were to be labelled '*un*satisfactory', perhaps some sharp-witted, and sharp-eyed, parents might begin to wonder whether it was the teaching that was unsatisfactory rather than the learning. With all independent schools, business is, after all, business. Money is an inescapable component of the equation.

However, on a purely common-sense level, it is difficult

to argue with the verdict that a report like this is just a mite skimpy, for all that it was typical of its era. And such reports continued for a long time. I was getting reports like this thirty years later, and, when I entered the profession, I was to see a lot more.

Does this mean that our predecessors in the common room were a negligent lot of smoke-soaked layabouts who could not wait to get back to their *Times* crossword or the bridge table? Not necessarily, no. There were just as many good teachers then as there are now, and they understood children just as thoroughly as the good ones do today. By the same token, I hazard the guess that, human nature being what it is, the modern profession is no more free from lazy teachers now than it was then.

Lazy or not, teachers in the 1920's did not usually have a great deal of space in which to operate. It is true that they normally had room for a couple of handwritten lines, and, to be fair, some of them used it. Incidentally, there was another factor, which continued to apply at least until the 1980's, and, for all I know, after that.

I worked in a comprehensive school in the 70's and 80's. This school prided itself on the fact that it provided a report of each pupil every half-term, besides the 'big' report that came at Easter or at the end of the summer term, usually just after the end-of-year internal exams.

That sounds fine, but it would have meant a much heavier load on teachers to prepare and write all these reports, in their spare time, *twice a term*. So our school authorities decreed that each child was to be issued with his report (blank). He or she carried it around with him (please assume 'or her'; I can't keep putting in both sexes), and handed it to the teacher of whichever class he was due to visit next. That teacher therefore started the lesson with a pile on his desk of thirty-plus report forms, which he had to have complete to give back at the end of the lesson (so that the pupil could do the same in the *next* lesson). A teacher had to collect the forms, collect last night's homework (and deal with excuses), give out some books, explain and set the work for the lesson, deal with questions, get their heads down, write over thirty reports (that is, award a grade and write some remarks), collect the books again, and see the pupils out – all in thirty-five minutes. Work out how much time he had for a detailed assessment of each pupil and his progress.

There were schools, we heard, who boasted that they provided reports on each and every child *every three weeks*. This was in the flood tide of comprehensivisation – if there is such a word. This was the time when the new gospel declared that we were all to be equal, that nobody was to be made to feel inferior, *that the pupil came first*. If you attended courses or conferences in the 1970's, there was always, near the end of the afternoon, some round-table discussion or 'forum' or 'brain-storming session' about something or other, and sooner or later an earnest member of the group would show his sharpness of mind and modernity and sympathetic nature by declaring, 'Well, I think it is time for us to remember that the children come first.' There is no answer to that. Well, there is, but it wouldn't have helped the proceedings along very much.

So one of the results of this 'the-child-comes-first' dogma was more frequent reports. Another was longer reports. Much was made of the monosyllabic reports I have described above. They were held up to ridicule and scorn, as if they were typical of an era which had produced child labour, public hangings, and the Spanish Inquisition. The audience was invited, by implication, to throw up its hands in horror at the mere mention of this ghastly ghost from the past, and to declare its born-again allegiance to the gospel of freedom, sympathy, understanding, and light that was being preached.

None of these prophets seems to have been alive to the possibility that longer reports did not necessarily mean better ones.

I have used this 1921 report described above to point out that it was, as I said, rather short, and could possibly have been fuller. But I have also seen many reports which nobody would have called wordy, but which displayed, on the teacher's part, fairness, sympathy, invention, understanding, and humour. I hope I have written some myself.

Try these for size:

'Cannot for the life of him see the point of effort.' Nothing but a statement of fact. It also implies, obviously, that the pupil is, by most standards, idle, that he will not have done enough work to pass the coming exam, and that, if he fails, he will have only himself to blame. There is no personal attack on the character of the child; he may simply have not woken up to the fact that effort is necessary for success. He may well wake up at a later stage (they often do). It may also be that he sees no attraction in the 'success' on offer. So why work for it? So in that case, the child is nothing if not logical.

'A fine exponent of the principle of economy of effort.' Again, a true statement. The boy is working well enough to pass the exam, but has other interests which engage his energy and desires, and which he wishes to pursue in the long term. He has in fact done what we are enjoined to do when faced with more than one task: he has 'prioritised'. He is intelligent and sensible enough to have worked out how much effort is required to pass, or to stay out of trouble, and has proceeded accordingly. Very shrewd of him. Shrewd of the teacher too to have spotted it. He has offered criticism and humour in the same phrase, and let the boy know that he, the teacher, has summed him up perfectly. Most boys accept this. All that, I put it to the court, is implied in that remark above.

'Has the makings of a good citizen.' This time the teacher has decided to offer a more generalised comment on what he considers to be the pupil's potential, and there is nothing wrong with that. After all, what is important in the long run is not what the pupil is doing in 3C or 5B now, but what he is going to do during the rest of his life. And it takes an experienced, perceptive teacher to be able to make a comment like this. He wouldn't do it every term, and there will be plenty of time in future terms to offer judgment on the pupil's command of French grammar or the theorem of Pythagoras. The chances are that he will never cast a glance at a past participle or a hypotenuse for the rest of his life, but he will have to become a citizen. A parent likes to read a compliment about his child's citizenly qualities; that's part of what he too is striving for.

Then there are the comments which may home in on a particular facet of the pupil. After all, you can't write an encyclopaedic, definitive character and output summary every single term.

I have written, more than once, about a boy, 'Absolutely charming. Idle, but charming.' Or the other way round: 'Idle. Absolutely charming, but idle.' The boy would know at once that I had summed him up, in the most friendly way. I had indicated that I knew I would never get any more effort out of him that I had been getting, and that I was prepared to live with this fact. He too would have to live with the fact that I had rumbled him. We understood each other perfectly. All the analysis of his 'ability to understand fresh concepts' or his 'detailed evaluation of sources' is not going to get past the truth that he is not going to do himself justice because he is idle. He knows it, and we know it, and he knows we know. We proceed from there. And a very happy relationship it is.

Or again, it is worth concentrating just once on a feature which has struck you forcibly during lessons: 'His concentration is fearsome. You can actually watch him listening to you.' Whatever the overall picture that one might try to paint elsewhere on the report, that fact deserves to be recorded. It could be the key to understanding the boy's success and progress. And it is a compliment after all.

While we are on the subject of compliments, there is a good case for passing one whenever the opportunity arises. The phrase 'Absolutely smashing' conveys the boy's progress and attitude, as well as indicating that the teacher is enthusiastic too, and the pupil has made him enthusiastic. It adds on the priceless feature of any good classroom relationship – the fact that pupil and teacher obviously strike sparks off each other. Which is splendid, and once again deserves to be recorded.

Then there is the pupil who grows on you. 'It takes a long time to get a smile out of him, but it is well worth the wait when you do.' Yet again, we are talking about a relationship, which the teacher has to work on. He naturally wants to record the fact that he has had some success. Any parent will want to know that his child gets on well with his teacher.

I am not making a case against all long reports. There are no doubt good long reports, just as there are good short reports. But I suggest that we have now passed from a 'short-report' era to a 'long-report one'. It is the fashion, the trend; it is the way things are going – for the time being. Reports have to be long.

So we have, for instance, '----- has produced some satisfactory work in [say,] Geography this term.' Now, beside the space for this report is printed the word 'Geography'. So why repeat it? We know already that this is a Geography report. When you assess what has actually been said about -----'s work this term, in what way does it represent an advance on the 1921 verdict, 'Satisfactory'?

All right, I am being unfair, because there are six more lines of report to come on -----'s Geography. But his name is repeated four times. Is this really necessary? Are we going to forget who we are reading about? (Incidentally, this boy's name was repeated in the whole report no fewer than forty times. And I wasn't looking for an extreme case; I had picked it totally at random.) Again, 'needs to make sure that he stays focused at all times and does not get distracted by others in the class'. Would 'inattentive' not be sufficient? Or even 'inattentive at times'?

It is indeed very easy to pick holes in almost anything if one tries hard enough, and it is *not* easy to compose scores, probably hundreds, of reports in a short space of time, especially when the fashion is at work to make us show that we are interested, and that we 'care'. If we are not 'caring', then my goodness, what sort of teacher are we?

But the effect, I think, has been to pressurise the conscientious teacher into composing lengthy sentences in the attempt to show that the pupil's report conforms with the current gospel of caring, of detailed analysis, of sheer volume, when a dash of daring and thought might have produced something more succinct, readable, helpful, and memorable.

What I am about to write is a world away from the foregoing examples, but I still maintain that it offers some insight, some humour, and some understanding. I had a bright eleven-year-old girl in a History class. She was new to the school, but took far less time to settle down than the average fresh arrival. She was sharp, able, and very willing to offer answers. Because they were usually right, she had developed a pretty healthy regard for her own ability, which she was intelligent enough to see was in advance of the average in her class. But modesty and tolerance of her fellow-pupil were not among her more observable talents. So I wrote at the end of her first term, 'An able little madam.'

Now, you may think that that was too clever by half, too slick, even unfair. I don't know. Perhaps if I had had to write her report today I would have been expected to write the previous five lines rather than the summary I actually did write. But I have to tell you that I met her father the following month at a parents' evening, and he laughingly informed me that I had got her dead right.

This quest for the snappy summary is of course a permanent temptation, and one must be watchful that the devil does not take over. It may do the teacher some good, and it may amuse the uninvolved reader, but it does not necessarily help the pupil. (It can also produce the most awful pitfalls. I have seen, on a Chemistry report, 'His spelling is disasterous' [sic].)

So while 'despite his natural levity, he invariably gravitates to the bottom' may provoke a smile, even with the boy himself, it does not contribute much to a perceptive analysis of his overall progress – though even this shows that he is a natural humourist and is no doubt the life and soul of the party, and every pack needs its joker.

I had a colleague who allowed his disapproval to show with a boy who had been persistently absent for the best part of the term: 'Who is this boy?' Again, not very helpful, but it did make the point that any assessment, long or short, was practically impossible because he had produced almost no work.

A useful trick, this – to display impatience, wariness, dissatisfaction, or whatever, by an oblique remark which gives no offence, but which, on reflection, conveys a useful truth. The court jester technique, if you like. So 'you always know he is there' can be taken more than one way, and the teacher can let it be known that he is well aware of those other ways. A sort of Delphic utterance – very convenient.

So where is all this getting us? Should reports be long or short? Because modern reports are twenty times longer, are modern teachers twenty times more conscientious, more understanding, and more effective than their forbears were ninety or sixty or forty years ago? Because reports now are more earnest and deadpan and chock full of words, does that make them more or less informative or stimulating than the snappy one-liners of a generation ago?

I'll tell you one thing: they ought to be personal. It

is arguable that a dimension has been lost as a result of the fact that teachers nowadays often type their reports – for filing on a computer, naturally. And they don't even sign them. That touch of individuality, that evidence of personal contact, has gone. Not a scrap of ink appears on that report. Pity.

Worse, when one reads daily of a new breed of anti-social beings called 'hackers', it does not seem beyond possibility that a resourceful pupil could get into the school's report domain and type his own (so long as he didn't give the game away by 'disasterous' spelling). He could even set up a business offering to type everyone else's – for a fee, naturally.

Which only postpones the answer to the question. For the life of me, I don't know. Do parents actually read these lengthy documents? The modern samples I have seen run to an average of over three pages of typed, single-spaced A4. We are light years away from 'an excellent report is all ways' or 'very satisfactory'. And, probably, a good thing too. But is all that verbiage worth all that effort – as I said, by conscientious teachers?

Take a look at them. They are just as vulnerable to the pressures of contemporary style and fashion as their predecessors were. Where we once had 'good' or 'steady progress' or 'most satisfactory', we now have words like 'focus', 'challenging', 'commitment', 'motivated', 'engaged'. We don't have 'very'; we have 'hugely' or 'massively'.

So have things really changed all that much? Will parents have learned to *interpret* reports just as they did all those years ago? Do they treat them with that mixture of eyebrow-raised curiosity, passing interest, tolerance, and scepticism that we all employ when faced with television adverts and newspaper headlines? One wonders.

As the man said, does size matter?

Rather than debating fruitlessly on the virtues of succinctness or prolixity, should we be concentrating on producing a report which shows perception, honesty, balance, fairness, perspective, *and clarity*? Which shows that the teacher understands, that he does not hope for the moon, that he does not regard a pupil's poor performance as some kind of personal slight on himself, and that he and the pupil are engaged on a joint project called education? Which treads a fine line between mealy euphemism on the one hand and calling a spade a bloody shovel on the other? Which can indulge in a gently humorous exposé of the pupil's shortcomings without falling into the trap of airing the teacher's ego on the other? Which displays a reasonable command of vocabulary, style, and punctuation by the people responsible for the standard of English *in* those reports? Which lets the reader know that the teacher is on the pupil's side?

A tall order.

A Japanese sword

THERE IS A STORY that the playwright W.S. Gilbert (the first half of the famous theatrical partnership) was walking down a corridor one day when a Japanese sword fell off the wall as he approached. I have not done scholarly research on this. Did it fall as he approached? Was it already lying there? Was it in his own house, or was it at some kind of exhibition? There was certainly a sort of Japanese craze at the time, and perhaps he was at one of the doubtless many oriental shows and events that must have fuelled or been fuelled by this craze.

At any rate, it put an idea into his head. Or perhaps it chimed with an idea which was already there. It is not always easy to pinpoint the exact moment when something 'came' to us. Things can lie dormant for years, and then need some charge or spark to activate them. Whatever it was in Gilbert's case, the result was *The Mikado*.

This somewhat laboured introduction is intended to show that unexpected results can come from the most unlikely material. What I am talking about here is the thing which pushed me into the teaching profession. Because push it certainly it needed to be. Like many young men of about twenty-one, especially those with training in the Humanities, I had not the faintest idea what I wanted to do when the Army released me from serving Her Majesty.

Well, I had ideas, but they were not practical. Just what was I going to do to earn a living? For the life of me, I couldn't work up much enthusiasm for business or industry. Certainly not the church or the law. And if there was one thing I knew I *didn't* want to do, it was teach. As I had nothing but a degree in History to offer, and a junior commission in the Army (which at that time was as common as sand on the shore), it was beginning to look as if the future was going to be pretty barren. Shop assistant, salesman, bar-tender, or busker . . . . the options were beginning to narrow somewhat.

Then GOC East Africa took a hand. He was the Japanese sword. A decree went forth from Nairobi that all British ranks serving with African regiments were to learn Swahili up to a certain certifiable standard.

What was I doing in East Africa? Doing my National Service. I had been lucky enough to secure a commission, and had been posted to the third battalion of the King's African Rifles. This was in Kenya. The sixth battalion, I think it was, was stationed in Tanganyika (Tanzania now), and the fourth in Uganda. I don't know where the others were.

Every junior officer was packed off to a three-week course in Swahili within a short time of arrival, and we spent a very comfortable time in the Equator Inn in Nairobi, whence we trooped off to lessons in huts and sheds somewhere or other to tackle the *lingua franca* of East Africa. African troops – *askaris* – naturally spoke their own tribal tongue, and they too learned Swahili when they entered the Army. And they learned it without the assistance of cosy three-week courses in the capital city, with lazy evenings courtesy of the Equator Inn.

I don't think British NCO's or other ranks had access to these courses either. They were thrown in the deep end. The result was that they learned a sort of pidgin-Swahili, or kitchen Swahili – the name and style derived from the relationship between the thousands of white farmers and businessmen on the one hand, and the legions of

On Teaching

assistants, cooks, cleaners, nannies, grooms, mechanics, and general dogsbodies on the other – all black of course. (The work 'black' is used simply to differentiate them from the whites; in fact several of the tribes had a dark or medium brown skin.)

The result was not what you might call satisfactory. The white half of the equation contented themselves with the knowledge that if they shouted and repeated themselves enough, and waved their arms about, they would convey the general drift of what they meant. If mistakes were made by the recipients of the orders, it could be convenient justification for the common assertion that Africans were often a little bit behind the door. The black half usually worked out what the 'bwana' meant, often long before he had convinced himself that he had conveyed the gist, and economic necessity (plus, quite often, some good manners) ensured that the situation would be tolerated for want of anything better.

However, some well-meaning senior administrator (who knows? perhaps a new-broom-sweeping commander-in-chief himself) decided that it was time for the British to show the way by raising the level of Swahili speaking among the white component of the Army in East Africa.

So the order was, I said, promulgated throughout the command. The British officers, NCO's, and other ranks were to get down to it and improve their tense prefixes and their adjectival agreements. This was to go right up to battalion commander level – lieutenant-colonels, no less – and right down to sergeants and corporals. Battalions were given so many months to achieve the desired standard, and exams were to be set. Mainly in oral work. I forget now how much time, if any, was given to a written exam.

That meant that commanding officers were to find

teachers. They were given no extra funds to hire such creatures. In any case, they must have been somewhat scarce, because nobody bothered very much about learning 'proper' Swahili.

So commanding officers started looking, and they started looking, as one would expect, around their own domain. It so happened that 2 Lt. Coates had returned from the Swahili course in Nairobi with a Grade 'A'. Fortunately, Swahili is a fairly logical language, and pretty phonetic (none of the nightmares of English pronunciation). Moreover, I had had experience of learning French, Latin, and Greek at school – even a few weeks' Spanish. And I was a bit of a swot. Hence the Grade 'A'. Had I known what it was going to let me in for, I might not have worked so effectively.

Anyway, you can guess the rest. My company commander was deputed to sound me out as to whether I thought I could teach Swahili to our sergeants and warrant officers once or twice a week after duties and before dinner. Having been on the receiving end of school education till I was eighteen, and having survived three years at university, I could be judged to have *heard* a good deal of teaching, but even I knew enough to know that I didn't know much about the doing of it.

However, when your company commander asks you whether you think you could teach a spot of Swahili to the battalion's NCO's, you don't rub your chin and wonder whether you might not be up to it; you say, 'Very good, sir. Right away, sir. Three bags full, sir.'

So I picked up the Japanese sword. What sort of Mikado came out of the decision is not for me to say. Anyway, it's a bit late now.

Doing the Reformation

IF IT IS ANY consolation to those pupils who have felt bored by their teachers, there are times (we hope not very often) when teachers can become bored with themselves.

I am not talking here of those unfortunate practitioners who are boring most of the time. Sadly, they exist in the teaching profession just as they do everywhere else. And, like all real bores, they have no idea that they *are* bores. No, I am concerned with sensible, hardworking, regular professionals who come up against the unavoidable problem of repetition.

Think about it. If, for example, you take the GCSE history class, you will have to face the task of conveying the mysteries of English foreign policy or the Poor Law or the Arab-Israeli conflict every single year, usually at about the same time of every year too, because of the exigencies of the timetable and the syllabus. If you are scheduled to take two or three GCSE history classes, say, in a large comprehensive school, you will have done those topics ten, fifteen, twenty times in less than a decade. And a teacher's career spans over three such decades, possibly four. It is not always a solution to change schools, because you could find yourself teaching another GCSE class anywhere else in the country, and if they are taking exams set by the same board as in your first school, you're lumbered, aren't you?

You are further restricted because of your desire to deliver the goods to a class whose members want to do well in those examinations, so i's have to be dotted and t's crossed. You can't cut corners with the material, not if you want to do your job properly.

Factor into the equation your level of tiredness at any particular time (and chronic fatigue is a perpetual hazard of full-time teaching), your recent recovery from a bout of flu, your domestic problems, your garage bills, your pettifogging director of studies, and a host of other annoyances, and you can be forgiven if occasionally you slip into the automatic pilot gear.

It is a result of professionalism itself. Familiarity with the work produces a sort of mental sleight of hand, and a series of tricks by which you achieve the desired set of results by less and less effort each time. Think of a familiar car journey you make, day in and day out. How many times have you arrived at your destination without any clear recollection of the details of the journey? The gloom merchants would suggest that it is an accident waiting to happen.

Fortunately, nasty accidents are not likely in the classroom, but the spectre of boredom can creep up out of the floorboards when you least expect it, and can cause a great deal of trouble if you are not vigilant. Fortunately, too, any teacher with a few years' experience has, if he is honest, been caught on the automatic pilot, so he is reasonably adept at spotting the signs when they recur. It is no great sin to become boring, any more than it is a sin to get tired, but it can be a sin if, having noticed it, we do nothing about it.

I used to catch myself when I was droning on about the usual material, say, when I was combining my 'lecture' with an amble round the classroom – you know, the relaxed, casual approach – 'Sir' letting it be seen that he is complete master of the situation, in total control, can do the lesson standing on his head.

On Teaching

There comes a moment when you can actually hear yourself talking; you are in their shoes – and it's pretty dire. You are moved to say to yourself, 'Coates, why don't you shut up!' So, as soon as possible, without giving anything away, you have to go to back to the desk, start them on some routine task which has to be done, and use the interval of peace thereby gained to think of something. Fortunately – for the third time – one skill a teacher learns if he is to survive is that of thinking on his feet, bringing up reserves from experience, 'coming up with something'. And, ideally, the joins shouldn't show.

I am able to report one occasion on which this happened, and on which too I was able to 'come up with something'. A lucky escape, if you like. All right – *another* lucky escape.

It was time for the sixteenth century. And you can't do the sixteenth century without doing the Reformation. You know? Martin Luther and the Pope and indulgences? (Don't you? Well, look it up, or the rest of this chapter won't make a lot of sense. I can't stop to explain.)

I was in full spate.

'. . . . so the Pope sent Tetzel round Germany selling indulgences. I'll talk about indulgences in a minute. [Miller is gazing bleakly out at the rain.] Then Luther – you remember what we discussed about Luther last week. [Thirty blank expressions. Well, twenty-three actually; the other seven are furtively putting finishing touches to some Algebra homework.] Luther decided to protest, and he nailed his arguments – theses, he called them – ninety five of them to the church door in his home town of Wittenberg. [Hetherington lifts his chin off his right hand and lowers it gloomily on to his left.] This was an act of such defiance that the Pope summoned him to a court, and, when he refused to withdraw what he had said, excommunicated him. [A minor storm erupts in the far left-hand corner because Drayton, while vacantly sucking his biro, has got himself a mouthful of congealed red ink.]'

The only consolation of the whole episode was that the resultant chaos relieved 'Sir' of the necessity, if only for the time being, of droning on about the same facts as he had done for the previous five years. It did not, however, relieve him of the problem of making the Reformation intellectually digestible, never mind enjoyable, to a class of thirteen-to-fourteen-year-olds.

Any teacher with only a smattering of experience knows that appeals to their better nature will cut no ice. Always proceed on the assumption that they haven't got any. If they really have, you have to allow it to come out in their own time; you can't wheedle it out like a snake-charmer.

Appeals to scholarly instincts can also be met with polite indifference. They may be there, hidden among the better natures, but again, you can't ask for them as a favour. They are not in the business of favours; they are there to be taught, and it is up to you to teach them.

No – the time has come for some low cunning. Think like a con artist. Con artists work on the principle that most adult potential customers are suckers if they think they are going to get something for nothing. Thirteen-year-old boys have their weaknesses too. All you have to do is locate them. Where are they vulnerable? What do they like doing? They like poking fun; they like pulling something to pieces; they like making jokes. They like nothing better than a little bit of iconoclasm.

On Teaching

You are teaching History. All right – give them some history to knock. And it so happened that I had to hand perhaps the greatest volume ever written on the subject of history-knocking. It had been, it was, and it remained, ever-present in my book cupboard. I refer, ladies and gentlemen, to a work that should be part of the essential equipment of any self-respecting History teacher. The authors, W.C. Sellar and R.J. Yeatman, met while studying History at Oxford after the First World War. The one became a teacher and the other a journalist. They began a long friendship, broken only by Sellar's death in 1951.

They published what became their best-selling book in 1930. It was a survey of the whole of English history, but not quite like any other survey of English history. Unlike its predecessors, it was based on a new assumption. Sellar and Yeatman argued that History is not what you ought to know; it is what you actually remember.

The result was a magnificent farrago of false assumptions, crossed wires, *non sequiturs*, jumbled reminiscence, useless knowledge, and rampant jingoism [England's remorseless progress towards becoming 'top nation'] which pleased everybody and fooled nobody. It was entitled *1066 and All That*.

The best way to convey the substance of it to those benighted souls who have been denied acquaintance with it is to offer a quotation. So here we go.

Here they are on the popular subject of 'Robin Hood and his Merrie Men':

'About this time the memorable [they only discussed 'memorable' dates and facts] hero Robin Hood flourished in a romantic manner. Having been unjustly accused by two policemen in Richmond Park, he was condemned to be an out-door and went and lived with a maid who was called Marion, and a band of Merrie Men, in Greenwood Forest, near Sherborne. Amongst his Merrie Men were Will Scarlet (*The Scarlet Pimpernel*), Black Beauty, White Melville, Little Red Riding Hood (probably an outdaughter of his), and the famous Friar Puck, who used to sit in a cowslip and suck bees, thus becoming so fat that he declared he could put his girdle round the Earth.'

Get the idea?

Now it so happened that a particularly quotable passage from the book concerned a topic this class had already dealt with – the Yorkist pretenders to Henry VII's Lancastrian throne in the 1480's and 1490's. This had come at the beginning of the school year, when everybody was fresh – both 'Sir' and the inmates – and the business of the 'Pretenders' had been pretty willingly mopped up. So, when I read out this piece, there were some healthy chuckles; they knew enough about it to get the jokes. I make little apology about quoting it all because it can almost stand on its own as a piece of humorous writing.

'English History has always been subject to Waves of Pretenders. These have usually come in small waves of about two – an Old Pretender and a Young Pretender, their object being to sow dissension in the realm, and if possible to confuse the Royal issue by pretending to be heirs to the throne.

'Two Pretenders who now arose were Lambert Simnel and Perkin Warbeck [this bit is quite right, but not the rest], and they succeeded in confusing the issue absolutely by being so similar that some historians suggest they were really the same person (i.e. the Earl of Warbeck).

'Lambert Simnel (the Young Pretender) was really (probably) himself, but cleverly pretended to be the Earl of Warbeck. Henry VII therefore ordered him to be led through the streets of London to prove that he really was.

'Perkin Warbeck (the Older and more confusing Pretender) insisted that he was himself, thus causing complete dissension till Henry VII had him led through the streets of London to prove that he was really Lambert Simnel.

'The punishment of these memorable Pretenders was justly similar, since Perkin Warmnel was compelled to become a blot on the King's skitchen, while Perbeck was made an escullion. Wimneck, however, subsequently began pretending again. This time he pretended that he had been smothered in early youth and buried under a stair-rod while pretending to be one of the Little Princes in the Tower. In order to prove that he had not been murdered before, Henry was reluctantly compelled to have him really executed.

'Even after his execution many people believed that he was only pretending to have been beheaded, while others declared that it was not Warmneck at all but Lamkin, and that Permnel had been dead all the time really, like Queen Anne.'

[The text is accompanied by a delightful illustration of the 'punishment of Lamnel (or Wermkin)']

So I proposed to take a leaf or two out of Mr. Sellar and Mr. Yeatman's book, and get them to have a crack at the Reformation. Once I had stated my intent, and given examples of Sellar and Yeatman's technique, and read a few more short passages from their book, they began to catch on. In short, what I wanted for their homework was a similarly garbled – or 'utterly memorable' – account of the Reformation.

Now, you see the fiendish subtlety of this exercise, don't you? They can't crack Sellar and Yeatman jokes about the subject unless they know what really happened.

Think of Tommy Cooper. He specialised in getting conjuring tricks wrong. To achieve that effect, and to make it look as if they had just that minute gone wrong by accident, he had to be a compulsive rehearser. And he was. He had to be a complete master of getting the tricks right before he could think about getting them to go wrong – to order. To put it another way, before he could do it wrong 'right', he had to be able to do it right 'right'.

So my iconoclasts had to make themselves masters of the main facts of the Reformation before they could construct a parody of it. Otherwise there would be no jokes, no ammunition. Here then was the con: they were induced to work quite hard at tackling the Reformation before they could indulge their desire to poke fun at it.

I could read out some of the best bits when I handed back the completed homework, we could all have a good laugh, and they would have learned about Martin Luther and indulgences pretty painlessly, without having had to listen yet again to my waves of oratory.

Naturally, I read out only the best bits; they were not all geniuses or budding Sellars and Yeatmans. But I got in enough good work to make me feel that the exercise had been worthwhile. And it was certainly different.

Judge for yourself:

'The Pope wanted to rebuild St. Peter's; money was needed, so people over-indulged themselves by eating Papal Bulls, which had been bitten by Tetzel flies.'

'[Luther] wrote 95 theories, the seventeenth of which caused Pythagoras to leap from his bath, shout 'Euclid', and write a set of very boring axles.'

'The Pope, who was in charge of selling Indulgences, issued Luther with a Paper Bull of Excommunication. He tore it up in the market place and nailed it in 95 pieces on the church door. . . . in a little town called Wittenfurt.'

'Having burnt the Papal Bull at the stake, he went on to preach at Wartburg, Wittenburg, and Waterloo (Wellington unfortunately was not there).'

'When Luther had finished his diet of worms and been sick, he was kept by the Saxon detector at a castle in Erfburg' . . . . 'and told to obliterate the Bible.' . . . . 'This led to a civic war.'

'At first the new monarch Henry was very popular as the inventor of Real Tennis. In Oxford, during the championships of this celebrated sport, he met and married Catherine of Aragon, widow to his dead brother Arthur, and aunt of [Emperor] Charles V. Erasmus, who was present, thereupon wrote the famous play *Charley's Aunt*. After eighteen years, Henry grew tired of her, and became infatuated with Anne Boleyn, the lady Real Tennis champion then.'

'Henry passed many acts such as the Act of Success, which meant Henry could not lose a game of tennis, and the Act of Apples, which gave him the first fruit of every apple tree.'

'Henry VIII began the Perforation in England. He was renowned for the acts and plays which were performed, and, I might say, usually passed, in Parliament. These acts were Good Things, because it taught the MP's Amateur Dramatics.'

'Henry made the Act of Superiority, in which England stopped being Catholic and started to be Top Nation.' . . . . 'Many people objected, especially a girl called Grace, and she went round destroying the surrounding countryside. This was called the Pillage of Grace.'

'But now, Henry found himself without churches or monks, so in order to put this right he built lots of new churches, and called them Churches of England. . . . So without knowing, Henry VIII had made the Reformation, which was a Good Thing.'

'Henry was also well known for all the Cardinals and head-churchmen he had in his reign. One was Wolsey, another Riley, another Austin. Luther was one of Austin's friars, but Henry did not know.' .. . . 'Sir Thomas More was made Chancellor after the General Election. [He was] a great friend of Oliver Twist, who once asked for him whilst in an orphanage.'

'Henry. . . . then became very fat and finally died of a surfeit of wives (he had 8), food, religion, and Papal Bulls.'

Some of them sustained the pace for several sentences:

'The Reformation was started by Martin Luther who was educated at Battenberg University. (The town of Battenberg had been made famous by Alfred the Grate, a memorable monarch, who fell asleep there while experimenting with his newly-invented coal fire and burnt the cakes. These cakes were then called Battenberg cakes.) One day when Luther was in his study studying, he saw a man called Tinsle, inventor of the same, indulging in selling indulgences to the people in order to raise money to build a Basket for St. Peter. But Luther, not being a great eater, refused to indulge and told Pope Leo the Lion what he thought of him (not much). Leo was very angry and sent a papal bull to Luther but as it arrived on a Friday, Luther was forced to burn it. When news of this reached Leo, he had Luther locked up in the Leaning Tower of Pisa.'

'The Reformation was the Religious Revolution (not to be confused with the Industrial one) of the 16th century A.D. . . . . Its leaders were Luther, Calvin, Zwingli, and the opposition leaders were the Popes (Leo the Xth, Julius Caesar the IInd, and Alexander the Great). Luther said the Church (R.C. of course) was wrong about religion and he was willing to damage a church door (a deadly sin) to make public his 95 reasons why.'

'Luther was the German leader of the 1917 Revolution and he based his election campaign on the selling of indulgences (pieces of paper allowing you to be excused from hard work half-way to Heaven or Hell) for money. In 1520 the Pope gave him a Papal Bull which he accepted graciously. . . . Next year he was ordered to go on a diet by his doctor (Dr. Albert Sweitzer) and to eat only worms for a few days. In 1546 he died (boo-hoo!). By this time the princes had picked sides – Lutheran, R.C., or B.C. So, in 1555, they made three treaties at Augsburg, Aprilsburg, and Septembersburg saying that provinces should follow their own prince (in single file if possible). . . . '

'Catherine the Harridan. . . . was Henry VIII's wife, but he preferred Anne Boleyn (memorable for dying twice, once beheaded and once when she fell off the Bloody Tower whilst admiring her head and not keeping her eyes on the wall). Therefore he wanted a divorce but the R.C.'s would not give it to him (a Good Thing) so he invented C. of E. so he could get it (a Bad Thing). This was the downfall of Thomas Wolsey, but the upfall of

Thomas Cromwell who is memorable for being the only man in English History to be the King's Secretary (250 w.p.m.) in 1534 and to execute King Charles V 115 years later. These were two of the many famous Toms of the time, two of the others being More and A Becket who was made a fake in 1538. Other famous Englishmen of the time were Archbishops Fisher, Angler, and Cranmer, who was burnt right hand first. One of Henry's last acts was that of dissolving and evaporating the monasteries into a crystalline form. His last act was to die, a Good Thing. With this event, the history of the Reformation came to a.'

And they still weren't finished.

As part of the fun in *1066 and All That*, the authors had inserted at intervals some revision tests. Again, I offer a few examples to give the flavour:

'Which came first, AD or BC? (Be careful.)'

'Has it never occurred to you that the Romans *counted backwards*? (Be honest.)'

'Have you the faintest recollection of Ethelbreth, Athelthral, or Thruthelfrolth?'

'What *have* you the faintest recollection of?'

'Why do you picture John of Gaunt as a rather emaciated grandee?'

'Who had what written on whose what?'

'Why on earth was William of Orange? (Seriously, though.)'

Once again, I'm sure you get the idea.

They did too. Try these for size:

'Do you think that Luther was really the Pope? (If so, do not bother to attempt the other questions.)'

'How was Luther too indulgent?'

'Can you remember any mention of Cranmer? (Think.)'

'Arrange Henry's wives in chronic order.'

'When was 1555? (Be very careful.)'

'Answer this question fully. . . .'

'Are you any the wiser after answering these questions?'

As I said, there was entertainment to be had, and I suggest they learnt a bit about the Reformation without too much grief. I think they caught the spirit of it very well.

I was pleased with the experiment, and some time later I tried a similar exercise with an imaginary conversation between the ghosts of Henry's wives. That went well too.

You can't be dashingly creative all the time, but it is very satisfying when something like this does go right.

Information in the rids

Just as any garrulous old lady can entertain you at the drop of a hat on the subject of her operations, so any teacher with more than five minutes' experience dealing with pupils from council housing estates has his or her own collection of 'absence notes' stories.

The title of this chapter comes out of a letter from a mum whose daughter had been absent the day before. (So she was prompt, and, as you will see, informative.) 'My daughter was absent yesterday, has I took her to the doctors, she had information in her rids [nasty!], which has to be treated with pain killers after ever [sic] meal, until it moves which will take time so the doctor says until then she has to learn to live with this discomfort, until she grows out of this or it might just go slowly away has [sic again] she gets older.'

To be just, a lady like this probably puts pen to paper very rarely, and she did cover the situation pretty thoroughly. And we all make mistakes. So, fair enough.

It is all too easy for frightfully well-educated teachers to enjoy a superior smile at the expense of someone who did not have the same opportunities as they did, or were simply not up to it. True. But now and again, one came across a train of absence notes, which, individually, fell under the heading of what I have been describing, but which, taken together, can constitute a sort of saga which could be worth recording, if only to chronicle the terrible misfortunes of the same pupil over an extended period. One's heart bled for him.

Let us call him Shane. In the school where I worked in the seventies, cohorts of boys enjoyed names like Shane and Kevin and Wayne, even Vincent and Francis. For the girls it was usually Sharon and Tracey and Tina and Deborah. We once had six Deborahs in the same class. Nothing wrong with any of these names, of course, but they did tend to come rather thick and fast. The Johns and Michaels and Davids and Margarets and Anns seemed to have taken a back seat.

Anyway, our Shane. He had trouble with nearly every part of his body, poor lad.

It started with the usual thing – an upset stomach. He was 'seeing the doctor today about his stomach' and Mother 'will ring again later'. I don't think she did.

This wasn't the first of Shane's crises with his innards. Only two months before we were phoned to be told that Shane had been seen by his doctor and been given medicine. He 'may have an ulcer', but will 'probably be back tomorrow'. Resilient, our Shane, if nothing else.

Resourceful too. Mother wrote a few weeks later to tell us that 'Shane was at home yesterday he went to the Doctors so while he was waiting he had his hair cut'. By the receptionist? By his Mum, in the surgery? Or was it common practice for patients to slip out of the waiting room on various grooming errands?

Further testimony to Shane's recuperative powers was a note to say that he had been 'sick all night' but had had 'a doze of something' and 'should be back this afternoon'.

It was only a matter of time before he was laid low by some virus or other. Sure enough, quite early in the academic year (September, actually – bit premature for viruses?) he 'is in bed with ever such a bad cold'. Mother was 'dosin' 'im up' herself with Disprin because 'if you go to the Doctor, they don't do nothing for a cold'. Well, she's right, isn't she?

But the real bane of Shane's life was clearly his legs and his feet. And it appeared to run in the family.

One day his sister rang to say that Mum was not well, and Shane had to stay at home to look after her as she had 'gone off her legs'.

Shane had already been a sufferer in this department. Mum phoned one morning to tell us that he 'can't 'ardly walk', so she was 'sending him to the doctor to get something to rub in'. Did he have to walk there, poor little devil, or did she send him in a taxi?

Shane was accident-prone too. One day his sister phoned up to say that her brother had been playing 'on a gate thing' and had fallen off. His toe was 'all swollen' and 'he can't come in' to school. The School secretary, suspecting something, asked why Mother wasn't ringing in as usual. Sister said that she (Mother) was at work. But, said the secretary, she had rung in before from the hospital, which was where she worked. Ah, no, said sister, she doesn't work there any more, so she can't get to a phone because 'she's on the leaflets'. Which of course explains it.

One day Mother decided to take a bull or two by the horns and evolve a strategy which would ensure the long-term health of her son's feet. She bought him a new pair of boots. He duly wore them to school. The following morning we had a phone call to say that Shane's new boots 'giv'd 'im 'orrible blisters', so he couldn't come to school. The secretary suggested plimsoles, but Mum said that they were very old and tatty, and in any case he would be in the next day because she had told him to soak his feet in salt water.

The efficacy of the salt water treatment was open to doubt, because I received another little note to say that Shane had not come into school the previous day because he had been 'in bed with his legs'.

But that was not the worst. On the first day of a new term I received this note from Mum: 'My son Shane was at home the last day of term as he had to go to the Doctor with his arm pits.'

There is no answer to that.

Expecting more

I FORGET NOW WHERE I read it, but some scholarly commentator or other, talking about Shakespeare, made the point that he (Shakespeare) was a great one for a spot of comedy in his dramas, even in the most deadly serious of them. Think of the gravedigger in *Hamlet*, or the vulgar buffoon Pistol in *Henry V*. It is hardly a world-shattering remark, and is no doubt a commonplace among actors and Shakespearean scholars, but it is nevertheless worth stating now and again among general readers. The Bard had cottoned on to the truth that it is asking a lot of an audience to absorb five acts of unmitigated horror and murder and base motives and war, even if the villains do get their comeuppance at the end. Mere retribution is not enough reward for two hours of gritted teeth.

Not only did he consider his audience's feelings. He had enough respect for them to appreciate that they could enjoy both comedy and tragedy in the same play; they could savour the whole gamut of the emotions in a single performance – even the noisy 'mechanicals' in the pit, the arsenal of heckle and catcall and nutshells and orange peel. They were emotionally mature enough to take in all of it, so long as they had some assistance from the author. A laugh steels you for the tragedy. Tragedy may be real and unavoidable, but comedy is vital if we are to survive it. In fact, our greatest actor, the late Laurence Olivier, went on record as observing that, when you boiled it right down, he wasn't sure whether comedy wasn't more important, in the end, than tragedy.

What has all this got to do with education? Two things, I put it to the court.

Firstly, the indispensability of humour. It is amazing what you can get a class to do if you have given them a laugh or two along the way. Humour is a wonderful fixative: it binds a class together in a shared joke; and it helps to seal a fact or a theory or a story in the memory. The teacher is lacking if he can not crack a joke, share a joke, and, sometimes, take one (so long, of course, as it is not unkindly meant).

Secondly, Shakespeare had, I repeat, respect for his audiences. Write well, construct a good plot with a good story line, create some good characters, lace it with some good jokes, and you can persuade those in front of stage (and, of course, in Shakespeare's time, round the sides of it and *on* it) to accept, and appreciate, almost anything, however apparently long-haired it may appear at first sight.

In the classroom, then, prepare your lesson in detail, with plenty of spare material in case they absorb it too fast; have clear aims, and state them; explain things well, frame questions which actually expect them to think instead of merely remember, make them laugh, and there is no end to what they can mop up, and enjoy mopping up.

Put more simply, make demands on them, and make them laugh. They are both forms of paying respect. The first shows that you think they are up to it; the second shows that you have given thought to helping them to go along with you, and that their appreciation means something to you.

Plays that are knocked out with merely the requisite numbers of murders or fights or bedroom scenes may be effective, clever, even successful, but they don't last.

Audiences will clap, but not for very long; they won't be content with a permanent diet of corn. There has to be something else. The trumpeter Winton Marsalis told a story about the wisdom of his father. When he, the teenage Winton, was dazzling his listeners with technical virtuosity, and getting cocky about it, his father brought him down to earth by observing, 'Son, if you play for applause, that's what you'll get.'

Similarly, with teaching, you must do more than throw facts at them, no matter how relevant or indisputable or unmissable they are. If you don't, all they will remember will be the boredom. It is worse still if you strew these facts before them as if you are throwing beads to the natives; to the boredom will be added resentment (see the chapter on 'Money for Old Rope').

It is all too easy to slip into this mood of assuming that 'they won't be up to it'. It is only a personal opinion, backed up only by personal impression rather than by statistics, that far too many modern dramas and documentaries on the television and cinema screen are the victims of this (in effect) cynical approach. No one 'shot' must last more than so many seconds, for fear that people will switch off. No adventure film is complete without yards of 'special effects', for fear that people will get bored with mere dialogue, even with a plot. Commentators and documentary presenters must be flown all round the world in order to stand in front of Mount Vesuvius or the Great Wall of China and come out with a one-liner (which, incidentally, they could quite well have done in a studio mock-up without anybody being the wiser). It is a whole culture of 'wham-bam and wow!'

Nor must anything be allowed to present too much

challenge to mental processes: boil it all down; simplify it; give it a 'modern' approach – with the inbuilt, implied suggestion that all previous approaches were not only 'old' (a crime) but 'old-fashioned' (even worse), and dryasdust, fuddy-duddy, 'superior', the result of blinkers caused by privilege, wealth, and condescension. It is effectively a form of inverted snobbery.

So Beatrix Potter stories must have their long words taken out, because children can't understand them – which is missing the point. The point is that they love the stories – every bit of them. They may not know what 'affronted' means, but they take it as part of the story, and like its familiarity, even if they do not fully understand that part of it. They will in time. They may not understand fully how the brace on Grandad's leg works, but it is part of Grandad, and he wouldn't be the same without it. It certainly doesn't bother them; it is familiar. They will sort out how it works sooner or later, and understand why he needs it.

I had trouble for years getting to the bottom of the two chapters in *The Wind in the Willows* entitled 'The Piper at the Gates of Dawn' and 'Wayfarers All', but I never wished to have them taken out or simplified. And I caught on to them in time.

Even Holy Writ has been subjected to this treatment. Shakespeare has had versions printed with the rude bits left out. Biggles books have been reissued with the dodgy racial bits changed. There are doubtless many other examples.

The modernisers and simplifiers miss another point too. There is no rule which declares that children, or adults for that matter, must be able to grab every single detail of a book or film or play straight off the bat. So far, nobody has suggested that Beethoven's Fifth Symphony ought to be 'made more accessible' by cutting out a scherzo here or a coda there so that audiences can 'get to grips with it' instantly.

So many of those who 'know better' for 'our good' fail to grasp the importance of the 'grapple' factor.

When I went to East Africa for part of my National Service, I was sent on a course to learn Swahili. We were taught 'straight', grammatical Swahili. Simple, maybe (the course lasted only three weeks), but 'straight', 'proper' Swahili. I learned in the course of it that there was another Swahili, the sort of Swahili that was used to deal with kitchen-boys and batmen and cleaners. (I should explain that Swahili was not often the usual language that Kenyan children learned at their mother's knee; that was the local tribal tongue. They learned Swahili when they got a job or went into the Army.)

So what they became used to in their day-to-day work was this kitchen Swahili – if you like pidgin-Swahili. I suspect this was (partly, at any rate) because their employers or superior officers (English) understood little better themselves. But, with a curious twist of self-justifying logic, they (the English) justified this use of kitchen Swahili by maintaining that this was all their domestic staff could understand. Proper Swahili – what was known as '*safi*' Swahili (the literal translation of '*safi*' was 'clean', 'clear', 'lucid') – was beyond them.

When I came back from my Swahili course, brimful of correct prefixes and accurate noun plurals, I was told, 'Oh, you don't want to bother with all that *safi* stuff. Waste of time. Half these askaris are straight off the tree.'

Being young and therefore knowing better, I persisted with my *safi* Swahili, and discovered, to my surprise and gratification, that I was getting through. Not only did they understand *safi* Swahili when I spoke it; they spoke it back to me. And I like to think that, because of it, I rose a little in their estimation.

Another example? One often hears that standards of punctuation are slipping, if not plunging. Apostrophes are scattered like confetti. Appreciation of the difference between a hyphen and a dash is fading. Semi-colons are an endangered species, and the colon is pretty well extinct. So why did a book on correct punctuation – Lynn Truss's modest offering entitled *Eats Shoots and Leaves* – become a best-seller? Somebody out there – in fact quite a few somebodies – still respects correct standards. It's a *safi* Swahili situation again.

A third. Take a look at any episode of the 1980's sitcom *Yes, Minister* – and its successor *Yes, Prime Minister*. Characters actually spoke to each other for minutes on end. Not a blue joke or a cliché or a four-letter word in sight. Some of the sentences were of Ciceronian splendour – and totally comprehensible, with the joke beautifully timed right at the end. It was impeccably researched. The characters were identifiable and memorable. The satire was deadly in its accuracy. It was simply so witty. It won awards.

Yet how many sitcoms today come anywhere near it for any of the above virtues? What was it that frightened the TV executives, despite the programme's evident success, away from doing anything remotely like it again? Yet there was the evidence, right in front of them – five series of it – that such ambitious ventures would work.

So – I repeat – make demands on them. Give them

credit for being able to grasp something, assuming of course that you are good enough ('good' meaning both 'competent' and 'kind') to explain it logically and thoroughly. If you start at square one, it is surprising how many squares you can proceed to and reach (and derive satisfaction from having done so).

For instance, don't be content with merely doing a 'project' on 'what it was like to be a medieval merchant', with drawings of dusty sandals and caravans of mules piled high with 'merchandise'. With a good class of twelve-year-olds, I was able to go into the niceties (all right, only a few niceties, but niceties nevertheless) of medieval economic theory; they were aware, for instance, of official papal doctrine on usury. They used illustrated reference books about medieval coinage and their comparative equivalents. They drew maps and read chapters which showed where amber or silver came from; how many rivers you had to cross going from Paris to Budapest; which countries had semi-permanent wars going on between Christian and Moslem; what was the average mileage you could expect in a day's travel; what the difference was between a market and a fair. If they wrote an essay about a medieval merchant, they had some meat to put on the bones.

Another example? Try castles. Castles are always a winner. They are big. They are obvious. They are simply 'there'; everybody has seen one at some time or other. Everybody knows what they are for – or thinks they do. Lots of kids have been 'over' a castle, so they start with some basic knowledge. Castles are in all the medieval text-books, usually with lavish technicolour illustrations. They have exciting things around them like battlements, arrow-slits, portcullises, drawbridges, moats. Adventures happen at castles – under the general heading of blood and thunder. At least that's the implication of all those 'exciting things'.

So – yes – they'll draw pictures and diagrams of castles till the cows come home, because of all the associated images that crowd their imagination while they're doing it.

But suppose we dig a little deeper. Suppose, for instance, we get them to consider how – and above all why – castles were invented. Because somebody had to. What was the military need? What was the social need? How did rulers come to be able to pay for them? What did early castles look like? Not like Caernarvon, that's for sure. So they grew, they changed, they developed. By an obvious process of logic, they declined too. They must have done, because nobody uses them for warfare now. So what happened? – when? how? why?

Lead a class on with the right questions, and they will tumble to the right answers. None of the concepts involved is beyond their comprehension or experience.

Now we're getting somewhere. So – let us consider – really consider – what are castles *for*? Well, fighting, obviously. Yes, but what kind of fighting? Clearly you can't take a castle into battle with you, so it will emerge that they are basically defensive. Build a castle big enough and strong enough, and the enemy won't dare to attack it. So, far from encouraging fighting, castles might have been put there to deter it. Common sense *if you really think about it*.

But we can do better than that. Suppose you have just conquered a country or a region. How do you hold it down? (Don't forget that the local population don't like you much.) How do you hold down a tablecloth on the grass at a picnic? You put stones at the corners and in the middle. So castles are strongpoints in a military occupation. Quite literally they hold a country down.

These castles are no good without soldiers to man them. Where do you put them? Somewhere safe. You can't billet them with hostile burghers and villagers; they would all get their throats cut as they slept. So a castle is a barracks.

Soldiers have to keep up their standards of efficiency. Recruits have to be taught their trade. They are not all fully-armed and fully-trained veterans, as they appear clattering up spiral staircases in Hollywood epics. They have to be fed; they have to be equipped; they have to be provided with weapons (which have to be maintained, even sometimes manufactured). So a castle is a training-ground, a food store, an arsenal, a workshop. It goes almost without saying that it is a huge kitchen, a stables, bakery, butchery, dormitory, and casualty centre.

Now suppose there is a war on. People get frightened. How can they protect their valuables? Yes, they can bury them. Many did; and for obvious reasons we shall never know *how* many. But many too put them in the most secure place they knew. So a castle was a safe.

Not only did a lot of people put their valuables in the castle. For equally obvious reasons, they put themselves there too, to avoid the hostile intentions of the invading army, never noted for its chivalry or respect for the rules of war. So a castle was a refuge. It needs very few questions from the teacher to make clear what the implications of that were for the castle's food supply or health or sleeping arrangements or toilet facilities.

Come at it from another angle. You are a king or a nobleman; you built the castle. (Incidentally, kings were not keen on too many of their noblemen building castles of their own. Because of their defensive strength, wayward nobles could break the rules, go to ground behind their drawbridge, and defy the king to do anything about it. Strong kings usually insisted on the principle of planning permission – a modern concept that turns out to have a very lengthy pedigree. That's another good trick – showing them that there is little new under the sun.)

So – when you visit the area, as you must if you want to make your authority felt (kings constantly travelled; some virtually rode themselves to death), where is the obvious place to stay? If you set up any kind of government process in the area, where is the best place to conduct business, keep tax money, store documents? If you dispense justice, where is the best large, enclosed space by means of which to overawe your miscreants? (Apart from the local cathedral, it was about the *only* large, enclosed space, and you could hardly hand out prison sentences from the high altar.) A castle therefore was also a residence, a state office, and a court – a convenient prison too.

Once again, all these concepts are well within a pupil's grasp, because, prodded with the right questions, he can work it out for himself. All it needs is for somebody to point his imagination and common sense in the right direction. And we all know, if you work something out for yourself, you are much more likely to remember it, because by that time you have forgotten the stimulus and persuaded yourself that you did it all on your own. Good for both memory and morale.

We still haven't finished. Let us take this a stage further.

Let us tackle the simple view of castles, the bit everyone thinks he knows – wars, sieges, attacks, the blood-and-thunder dimension.

Once again, *think*. Is it really like that – *all the time*? Are invading armies always going to march right up to a castle, shoot a few arrows, rumble up a couple of siege towers, and pour hundreds of roaring troops over the walls? And even if they did, would your average castle crumble before something as predictable as that? Would the men inside not have made some preparations?

If you frame your questions sensibly, you can get them to work out a great deal before they turn a single page of text-book.

For example, if you were the garrison of a castle, how would you prepare for a possible attack? Sheer gumption – you'd send out scouts to find out where the enemy army was, how strong it was, how fast it was moving. You would clear the trees and other cover all round the castle, to give a clear view. You would top up your stores of food and weapons and ammunition. You would check, and double-check, the reliability of your water supply. If you are going to pour boiling oil on to the heads of the scaling ladder parties, you have to make sure you have the cauldrons, the ropes and tackle to tip them, the fuel to light the fires, the oil itself. None of these things just happen, as in a few closely-edited seconds of Hollywood epic; they have to be planned.

And what about your problems with the crowds of refugees pouring in from the surrounding countryside? How are you going to feed and house them? How do you keep them out of the way when the fighting begins? What do you do with all the children?

Think ahead. Is there any chance of being rescued? Is there a relief army on the march? How do you make and keep contact with it? How are you going to keep up the garrison's spirits, especially during the period of waiting? Sustaining a castle in an invasion, like life in the trenches during the First World War – indeed like life in any war – is nine-tenths boredom and worry and not knowing, and only one-tenth action and danger. Children can readily understand all this.

Now look at it from the other side. You are going to attack a whacking great big castle. What – on earth – are you going to do? Another trick is to get them to think simple. Faced with an obstacle – never mind where or in what century – what are the three basic ways of dealing with it? Exactly – you go through, you go over the top, or you go underneath.

Now we have some hooks to hang the details on. So battering rams and catapults make sense. So do ladders and grapnels and tall siege towers. Less well known, but pretty obvious when you begin to think about it, is, quite simply, digging a hole. Underneath the walls, to make the walls collapse. Tedious, but it could be very effective, as prisoners of war found all over Germany in the Second World War (all right, so they were trying to get *out*, but the basic idea was the same – the circumvention of an obstacle by going underneath it – so things don't change much). It was known as 'mining' in the trade. Defenders had an answer to that – counter-mining; you dug a tunnel under the attackers' tunnel and tried to make *it* collapse.

By this time you have got across the point that castle sieges were not all about gallant assaults on the walls.

A lot of the work was much more tedious, boring, and mundane than that.

Less spectacular still was doing even less – simply sitting there and waiting for the garrison to run out of food and surrender. Once more, with questions, you can elicit most of this from a class once you have got them thinking.

Now get them to ponder that very inactivity. What are the problems of looking after an army which is sitting down outside a castle and doing nothing? Discipline, morale, weather, food, camp hygiene, disease – it is all simple if you give it thought. Oh – and they probably don't know where the relieving army is either.

If you are lucky, and strike the right chord with some imaginative questioning, you can arrive at yet another method – cheating. Pay a traitor to open a strategic gate at a pre-arranged time. (This in fact was the most common way of getting into medieval castles – but it wouldn't have made a very good epic, would it?)

One could go on. One is bounded only by the strictures of the timetable and the need to get on with the prescribed syllabus. A class can get their heads round pretty well all of this, because it is not, as they say, rocket science, but, for the umpteenth time, common sense. You have got across the point that the people involved in all this were not shadowy figures from a vague past composed of static tableaux, but ordinary human beings trying to deal with a set of very real problems which are easily understandable even today. And you have brought it alive with details which they can appreciate and sympathise with – and interpret. And write about. If you make them the commander either of the attacking army or of the castle (or of the relieving force), and ask them to frame plans, their problem is not what to put in but what to leave out.

That is what I mean by asking a lot of them. Expect more. You very often get it.

An extinct species

It often comes as a shock when a person of, shall we say, 'mature' years wakes up to the truth that something he has lived with for so long that he had accepted it as a fact of nature is on the contrary totally unknown to over half the people around him.

For instance, take any group of twenty-somethings and try them out on Greta Garbo, Gorgeous Gussie, Mr. Molotov, the Piddingtons, Gordon Richards, Screaming Lord Sutch, Ras Prince Monolulu, Juan-Manuel Fangio, King Farouk, even Charlie Chaplin. I was once sharing a conversation about cricket with a contemporary (not long ago), and we fell to discussing Don Bradman. A boy who had been listening attentively (because he was a keen cricketer himself) said, 'Who's Don Bradman?' Not long ago a 'quality' Sunday paper journalist told the story of two thirty-year-old Canadian fellow-journalists he had met who genuinely thought that the Vietnam war was the last chapter in the Second World War. Journalists!

You can never take anything for granted. So when I say 'Secondary Modern School', the next thing I shall have to do is explain what it was.

In 1944, that is, before the War ended, Mr. R.A. Butler, in the Coalition Government, secured the passage of his Education Act, which was going to build the education system of a sunlit-uplands post-war future – with all the glossy rhetoric that that implied about fairness and opportunity and progress and promised land and everything else. Utopia would be a Slough of Despond by comparison.

What did it do? It divided the country's secondary education system – as Caesar did with Gaul – into three parts. Every primary school pupil would take an exam at the age of eleven – the famous (or notorious, depending on your point of view) 'eleven-plus'. The exam itself was not new; pupils had been sitting for the 'scholarship' since the first decade of the century. What was different was that more careful provision was to be made to allocate the 'right' children to the 'right' school. For the high-fliers, the ones who passed the eleven-plus, or the scholarship if you wish, there would be a place at a local grammar school. For those who were not in that rarefied academic bracket, but who clearly had some educational potential, there were to be the technical colleges – the 'tech's.' For everybody else, there was to be the 'Secondary Modern' school.

It is not my intention to open a debate about the value of the eleven-plus, the ethos behind the 'Tech.', or the apologies made for the fairness of the 'Sec.Mod'. I am simply trying to explain how the 'Sec. Mod.' came into being.

On the face of it, it might appear that they would come to be regarded as the pits, the end of the line, the dumping-ground, whatever unpleasant epithet you may like to lay your tongue to. Not necessarily so. I have spoken to several people over the years who said that they had received some good training at their local 'Sec. Mod.', and they had nothing but good memories of it.

I also worked in one, and I should like to record that there was no feeling of negativity about it, no 'hard-done-by', 'we've-had a rough-deal' attitude among either pupils or staff. The buildings were clean and smart. The equipment – so far as a young teacher with only a year of experience behind him could tell – was up to scratch.

There was adequate space, a good games field, and very acceptable kitchens.

The children did not look scruffs. General manners and deportment were well within the bounds of good taste. Dammit, there are many products of the poshest public schools whose contempt for authority goes well beyond that of your average tike. That is not to say that our lot were all angels; of course they weren't. But, looking back, only one boy stands out in the memory as being really unpleasant; and I fancy, if I had had the experience of thirty years behind me instead of the one I had at the time, I could probably have handled him better.

The staff looked the part. Suits were, if not universal, pretty common. If not, it was bound to be sports jackets. Ties were certainly universal. Shoes were clean. There were not the tieless rugby shirts, baggy cords, clumpy sandals, and bitty beards that spread like foot and mouth among the profession *after* the advent of the comprehensives.

This is only anecdotal evidence, but my impression, from various conversations, is that for a decade or two after the War, discipline in sec.mod. schools may even have *improved*, because of the return of so many ex-servicemen to the profession – gritty men in their thirties and forties with a depth of experience beyond their years, who were simply not going to tolerate bad behaviour, bad manners, or bad attitudes. A colleague told me of a school where he had worked – a sec. mod. – where no boy would dream even of going about the place with his hands in his pockets. So, whenever the Good Old Days changed to the Rot, and discipline went to the dogs – if indeed they ever did – it wasn't because of Mr. Butler and his Education Act.

I may have been lucky, I don't know. I have no doubt that there were many schools which really were the pits, the end of the line. (One must remember that there must have been some seedy grammar schools and corrupt public schools too, because human nature does not change.) But that was not my experience with the sec. mod. I worked in.

The surprising thing was that they could not afford to be particularly choosy with the staff they engaged. When I appeared on the education scene in the late 1950's, the shortages of teachers, it seemed, were dire. When I had decided to go after a job in the Home Counties, all I had to do was choose from four closely-typed, double-sided foolscap sheets of vacancies. I could practically choose my street.

To my surprise, my very first application was acknowledged by an invitation to attend for interview – for head of department! I had only been teaching for about six months.

Resplendent in best suit and best manners, I duly presented myself before the usual array of local worthies behind a rampart of tables in some 'centre' or other. I have no recollection of what was said. All I remember was being invited back to the school for lunch while they deliberated on the doubtful potential of this green young man for fulfilling the duties of Head of History in a Secondary Modern school of over four hundred pupils. They would let me know their verdict after lunch.

I was met at the school by the deputy head, who took me into the dining room and introduced me to the members of staff who were already at the table. Probably because of the adrenalin flow caused by the stress of the interview, I was still a little 'high', and I talked rather more than I should have done – right through the first course and then through the dessert. The deputy head, who had long since finished, lit his pipe, and watched me slightly amusedly through the smoke.

When I had at last talked myself to a standstill, he took his pipe out of his mouth and said, 'I think you'll get the job.'

The pit gaped at my feet. Blindly and blithely, I jumped in.

'Why?'

'Because,' he said, 'you're the only applicant.'

He was right. I was, and I did.

I soon grew a great deal more respect for the shrewdness of this gentleman, He had been in the school for over twenty years, maybe thirty. He had risen from the ranks. He knew the school, the area, and the local families through and through. Nothing surprised him, nothing upset him, nothing threw him. He rarely had to raise his voice, whether in teaching or in dealing with discipline in general. No boy was rude to him.

His job fitted him as neatly and comfortably as his tweed jacket and his pipe. I once asked him why he smoked one. He paused, thought for a minute, took his pipe out of his mouth, and said, 'I suppose it's because I don't like not smoking one.' It was certainly as much a part of him as his calm manner and his reminiscent chuckle. He once told me that, in his younger days, when he and his wife were struggling to make ends meet, what with the mortgage and everything, he always managed to find enough every week to buy two ounces of what he called 'Cob Nut'. (I had never heard of this brand before, and I have never heard of it since.) In the summer term, he would often tell us that he had got up at about five o'clock because he simply couldn't stay in bed a moment longer. Then he would go into his garden and spend a blissful hour and a half hoeing or weeding or potting or whatever it was.

He was that human rarity – a man who was completely at ease with himself and with what he was doing. And God knows, as deputy head, he had his crosses to bear. Chief among them, I should think, would have been the Headmaster.

I never got to the bottom of this man. I never worked out what his method was. I couldn't decide whether or not he was real. On the face of it, he seemed an unworldly buffoon, totally out of touch; yet he was able to keep order, and he taught Maths, very successfully so far as I was aware. And he was, as I said, the Headmaster. And yet. . . .

When I presented myself at the school for the start of the autumn term, I took the precaution of coming in on the day before – for reasons of good manners, common sense, and the vital need to learn at least some of the ropes before being overrun by hordes of boys. To my amazement, I learned that the Headmaster was on his way back from his summer holiday. Nearly eight weeks in which to take a holiday, and a school of over four hundred pupils to prepare a new academic year for, and he wasn't there.

Of course, his deputy, with his pipe, was. Mr. Goldman (not his real name) did all the things that needed doing. Puffing patiently and rarely raising his voice. In this he was aided by the school secretary, Mrs. Fallon (not her real name either).

Mrs. Fallon was my first experience of a school secretary, as a teacher, that is. I had known a school secretary during my time as a pupil at my grammar school, naturally, and I was both wary and respectful. With good reason; one ticking off she gave me when I was ten remained in my memory in letters of fire for decades. But now I was a member of the profession, I thought; things were going to be different.

Almost within hours, I realised (thank God) that I would have to be wary and respectful of this lady too. She was rather more benign in manner than the dragon at my grammar school, and, when she presided at the table and received the staff's weekly dinner money, she called everybody 'dear' as she wrote the receipts. But fortunately I had just enough wit to see that the cold steel lurked underneath. I was far too young and callow to understand the depth and extent of Mrs. Fallon's contribution to the smooth running of the school, but at least I grasped enough to see that she was indeed important. It was a lesson that I took to heart. At every school where I subsequently worked, I made it my business to get in the good books of the school secretary. (The other functionary whose goodwill was paramount was, and still is, the school caretaker. These two are the great facilitators. With them all things are possible; without them you will barely get to first base.)

Any headmaster depended, of course, on his deputy head and his secretary, but I soon began to suspect that this headmaster depended on them a great deal more than was usual. When events loomed, and it became evident that some organisation was required, some initiative, some simple paper work, it was rarely forthcoming. One of his favourite sayings was 'I find these things organise themselves'. What he meant was that, if he left it long enough, some willing and conscientious underlings – in this case the deputy head, Mr. Goldman, and the School Secretary, Mrs. Fallon – would step in at the eleventh hour and put the show on the road. Because they were good at what they did, the event usually went off well enough, and our Headmaster was thereby vindicated in his philosophy. So he never felt the need to correct it.

The same thing happened with preparing the playing field for an athletics meeting. I don't think we had a proper groundsman; the council couldn't afford it. That did not faze our Head; he knew things 'organised themselves'. So once again, members of the P.E. staff got to work at the last minute with the flags and the measuring tape and the white markers. The meeting was a great success, and HM. went about the field patting heads, twirling his moustache, and talking benignly to parents about the school he was so proud of, and heaping praise on his loyal and hardworking staff. What a wonderful man.

Yet look at him in his day-to-day business, and he seemed so unworldly – even to a twenty-four-year-old still wet behind the ears. He was a keen Morris dancer, for a start. This is quite unfair, but I find it difficult to take Morris dancing seriously. I know it is absorbing for the converts, and it is deep and subtle and goes back a long way and is not easy to perform, but when a young teacher discovers that his Headmaster is an enthusiastic Morris dancer – all those knickerbockers and ribbons and sticks – well, it just does not sit well with the concept of stern authority. Worse still, he kept a large photograph of himself, in full regalia – and he was a big man – on the wall of his office. Your attention was drawn to it as if by hypnosis every time you went in there.

When that was added to his apparent impracticality – his near-posthumous arrival for the start of the new term and his unwillingness to organise in advance – you began to wonder.

Then there were his assemblies. All headmasters read out news of sporting and academic successes, and everybody gives a perfunctory round of applause. But this man laid on such a thick spread of sugary comment about pride in the school that you felt that it would be only a matter of time before some boy made a rude noise or otherwise disturbed the proceedings.

Many heads today find it difficult to get boys to sing hymns. Some have abandoned the struggle altogether. Others have special assembly 'practices' where they do little else but go through the hymns and get them used to the tunes and to making at least some kind of noise. Not enough for this man. Not only did he get them to make a good deal of noise with the hymns; he got them to sing – I repeat, *sing* – the Lord's Prayer. Can you imagine – over four hundred boys, with few academic prospects, and little musical education, standing together in an assembly at nine o'clock in the morning, *singing the Lord's Prayer*. I don't know how the other staff felt, but it made me cringe. It was too tacky for words. But, incredibly, the school took it, and duly delivered. How did he do it?

As I said, I was a new young teacher; there may have been a lot going on that I missed. But my overwhelming impression was that it was Goldie who was running the school, ably assisted by Mrs. Fallon, and a batch of well-seasoned staff who did whatever was necessary within their own spheres. (It was not the last time I was to witness this phenomenon.)

I suppose, looking back, I was lucky to come across so many mature teachers so early. It was not that they all used to take me on one side and pour good advice into me; nor did they pontificate about education to anybody who was around. They did not go on about having a vocation. I do not recall any of them expressing regret or frustration that they were working in a measly sec. mod. They did not moan about authority or the idiots in the education office – though I daresay the quirky behaviour of the Headmaster must have provoked a seditious thought or two.

They just got on with the job. They knew their subject, and they were obviously deeply experienced at it. They all kept good order. It was a fine example to a young beginner.

I never dreamed of addressing any of them by his Christian name. It was 'Mr. This' and 'Mr. That'. How I envied their easy manner with the deputy head, calling him 'Goldie'. It was an Olympian familiarity to which I hardly dared to aspire – though it is true that relations among staff were a great deal more formal then than they are now. At my first school the year before I had addressed young primary teachers the same age as myself as 'Miss'.

So Mr. Hubbard ruled in his Woodwork room; and Mr. Essery (hearing aid and all) beavered benignly away in his laboratory; white-haired Mr. Carroll purveyed his lessons in English with sublime humour and detachment; and Mr. Chaloner wielded a rod of iron in his Metalwork foundry. Mr. Chaloner, in particular, with his shiny bald head and his slightly protuberant eyes, must have scared the daylights out of junior boys at least. He certainly made me swallow once or twice, till I got used to him. To be fair, I did discover quite soon that he was good company, a humorous realist, and eminently pragmatic.

Gaining in confidence, I once asked him why he exerted such fearsome control. Wasn't it going over the top just a bit, I ventured. He turned his fearsome orbs on me.

'Remember what I teach. I've got lathes and drills and furnaces in there. What would happen if I relaxed for a minute?'

What indeed.

Not all the staff were such paragons of course. There were the young ones like me; another fellow about my own age started at the same time as I did. His subject was English. There was a supply teacher who came in quite a lot (remember the teacher shortage I spoke about; supply teachers were in great demand). I am bound to have forgotten one or two.

There were also the eccentrics, the ones who didn't quite fit. Most common rooms have them, though perhaps they are not quite so thick on the ground as they used to be.

We had a professional musician for a start – violinist. That is, he had been a professional violinist, but, like so many before and after him, found that the living was too precarious, particularly if one had a wife and family. So he resorted to teaching English. I have no evidence as to how good or effective his teaching was, but my impression from what he said in the common room was that his heart was not in it. It was a second best, a make-do. He rarely refused an agony call from a distraught orchestral manager to fill in for a player who had suddenly fallen ill just before an evening concert.

'Dropped everything at an hour's notice yesterday. Had to go the Abbeyworth Hall to do the Beethoven five.' Oh, yes, he was that good. He taught the violin too, outside school hours. A thankless task, one would have thought. Not with him. He may not have been the most dedicated English teacher, but he was a dedicated musician. And, while I was there, he had a prize pupil – a lad of about fourteen, who was clearly several cuts above your average schoolboy fiddler. This boy was serious; he really meant it. And it showed. I think it was one of the most refreshing draughts of pleasure for our English teacher in an otherwise pretty arid desert of philistinism. His progress was testimony to the hard work of both teacher and pupil, in a school which had none of the privileges and clout of an independent establishment.

Then we had a Geography teacher who was passionate about film-making. I was a bit of a film buff, and enjoyed our conversations about the cinema. Up to then I had simply sat in the stalls and soaked up whatever went on in front of me. Thanks to him I began to understand what people like producers and directors and editors do. Like all enthusiasts, he loved talking about his obsession.

It was thanks to him too that I became aware of the National Film Theatre. He was a qualified film projectionist, and used to make a pound or two extra working in the box at the NFT. He talked about it, and some time later I took the plunge and paid my subscription to the National Film Institute, I think it was. I used to receive a no-nonsense magazine reviewing all the latest films, and

I had access, naturally, to the NFT itself. Saw some very interesting stuff too.

Our Geography man didn't get much chance actually to make films, though there was one project I remember he became taken up with. It was a documentary about Hyde Park. Apparently, his part in it was to sit up in a tree with a movie camera for hours on end, filming what went on beneath him on the grass and round about, regardless of what it was.

They must have shot miles and miles of film, and the task of editing would have been monumental. I don't know if a finished article ever came out of it. Imagine – all those hours, up there in the branches, in all weathers. There were a few compensations: he used to hint at some enhancement of his education provided down below him by a lot of urgently unaware courting couples.

Finally, there was our PE teacher. Bluff, amiable, good company. Alas, not the most dedicated of his trade. He used to take lessons in the gym *sitting down*. He was a big, strong man too, and he was an athlete of county standard. But my abiding memory of him is of teaching PE from a chair. He was six feet three if he was an inch, so *he* didn't have any trouble keeping order either.

When he heard that I was about to accept a post in a grammar school, his advice was brief and to the point: 'Don't.'

When I asked why, he said, 'They do homework in grammar schools – miles and miles of it. Is that what you want – all that marking?'

I think I must have baffled him somewhat. Here was this young man, who had, prematurely, acquired a plum position in a nice comfortable little sec. mod. – head of department and all. He seemed, after a year, to have got the job nicely sewn up, and had a lovely thirty years of comfort spaced out before him. And here he was, trying to get out of it and into some hothouse of eggheads where they did endless extra lessons and out-of-school activities and homework (which all had to be marked). He shook his head sadly.

Was this a typical staff from a typical English secondary modern school common room? I wouldn't know; I never became an inspector, and I never worked in another 'sec. mod.' All I can say is that they welcomed me; they tolerated my inexperience; they were easy to work with; and, so far as my limited knowledge allowed me to judge, they seemed to be running a pretty effective establishment. They were, as a group, positive, and they knew where they were going. I detected little sign of hard-luckery or rough-dealery. (Ironically, the only one who was making regular efforts to get to another type of school was me.)

They offered proof of the fact that any school can work, or be made to work, if enough competent and sincere teachers believe in them sufficiently to spend a large slice of their professional life working in them. So perhaps the 'sec. mod.s' weren't so bad after all. Yet within twenty years or so of the passing of Mr. Butler's act, the reformers were working to get rid of them because they were blocking children's advancement. The 'sec. mod.' was a dead end. The eleven plus was an elitist plot to blight children's lives at a tender age. The answer was, of course, the comprehensive school.

So the 'sec. mod.', which had been part of the great pioneering achievement in 1944, the great open way to fairness and an education tailored to the needs of the children, was, within two decades, part of the barrier to progress. The flagship of opportunity had become the decaying hulk of frustration blocking the harbour exit to the great sea of success.

By the same token, and at roughly the same time, the grammar schools were castigated as being academic hothouses teaching subjects that were no use (like Latin and Greek), nestling behind their Maginot Line of the eleven-plus which was keeping out the bright working-class child who had not had the same opportunities.

So those teachers I knew in my sec. mod. were told, in effect, that the school they had been serving was no longer fit for purpose. At the same time, staff in grammar schools were warned that, if they wanted to survive in the 'real' world, they would have to lower their barricades, and their sights. Both sets of teachers were, in effect, not going to be allowed to do the job they had worked so many years to perfect. And told, as often as not, by angry doctrinaires and political do-gooders who had clawed their way into positions of authority which enabled them to dictate to a profession in which very few of them had classroom credentials – like the vengeful cabinet minister who was credited with saying that if it was the last thing he did, he would kill off the effing grammar schools.

It is ironic that the remedy for all these alleged evils – the comprehensives – have themselves not had a particularly long or successful life either. At least that would appear to be the case, when we hear of so many schools now being set up by committees of parents and other benefactors; of the Government encouraging the founding of such schools; of the rising numbers of parents who try to get their children into the independent schools; of a cabinet adviser referring breezily to 'your average bog-standard comprehensive'; and to the browbeating of the top universities to make sure they take more pupils from these comprehensives, whether they are of top potential or not, because it is 'fair'. Is that not an admission that the 'comp.'s' have not delivered?

Well, ours is a free country, and people must be allowed to have their own points of view. But it seems a pity that the people who were, and are, to be most affected by these momentous changes were, and are, usually the very ones who have never had their points of view consulted – the teachers, the parents, and the children.

Are you mekkin' eyes at me, Bernard James?

THEY WERE SO DESPERATE for teachers when I came along that when I went to see the local Chief Education Officer on the Monday, I started work on the Tuesday. No checking of references (I had none). No discreet phone calls to previous employers (there weren't any; I had just come out of National Service). No forbidding table-ful of local commissars to interview me. Just a chat across the CEO's besieged desk through the cigarette smoke, and I was in.

I had never taught before, apart from some recent after-hours Swahili instruction in the Army (where I outranked them all, so I had no discipline troubles). I had no teaching diploma. The school was in the north of England, which was injun country to this unlearned southerner. It was co-ed, and I knew next to nothing about girls, full stop – much less *teaching* them. The age range was from 8 to 15 (that was the leaving age then), and the last time I had been in a primary classroom was when I was 10. It was a tough school in a tough area in a tough city. Oh – and my first day was 5th November. Some start.

Why did he take me on? I had told him that I had a Cambridge degree in History, and he accepted it. And, as I said, he was desperate. Just how desperate I discovered when I met two more recent arrivals on the staff on my first day; they had just left the sixth form in their respective schools. Not only did the school not have its full complement of qualified teachers; it did not even have a headmaster. As far as I could gather, the previous incumbent had left suddenly at the end of the summer term; they were right into November and still had not found a replacement. The deputy head was running the place.

Running it pretty jolly well, however, so far as I could see, with my innocent eyes. Jack Milford had no difficulty keeping order. And he taught Maths of all things. Hardly the favourite subject of pupils like ours. Or anybody else's, come to that. He never lost his temper. I cannot recall his raising his voice. He was always dressed in a suit, waistcoat and all. His handwriting on the blackboard was a model of what it should be. He had been teaching for over thirty years – a whole lifetime to me.

How much he must have seen. He told me once that he remembered, as a young teacher, seeing children coming to school barefoot. It was the first of many shocks I received. Put that together with the bleak streets, the terraces, the universal greyness of a city built on woollen mills, the smoke and the grime, and I could perhaps be forgiven for feeling that I had just joined the world of Dickens or Arnold Bennett.

This impression was reinforced when I made the acquaintance of the school's oldest member of staff. Mr. Smith had begun his teaching career during the heady days of the Russian Revolution! (A century means almost nothing; here am I, in the second decade of the twenty-first century, and I can claim to have worked professionally with somebody who was teaching in the second decade of the twentieth.)

I soon saw things which I had blithely imagined to have disappeared in the nineteenth. Which only shows how ignorant a young man with a degree and an Army commission under his belt can be.

For example, I made the acquaintance of the nit lady.

I was appalled to discover that her trips were not only desirable and preventative, but necessary and remedial. Clearly, soap and water were not familiar features of a lot of local households. Overcrowding, ignorance, and neglect completed the equation. I soon learned that there were certain pupils over whose heads one did not lean too closely when one was looking at their work.

There was no question of a school uniform. Many of the smaller ones, it seemed, hardly ever wore clothes that had been bought for them. Bought for older brothers and sisters, yes, but not for them. The poorer ones rarely enjoyed the luxury of a top coat; they were out in the frost and fog with frayed jumpers out at the elbows and the hems. I was told stories (though I did wonder at the time whether I was being subjected to a spot of dramatic licence and hyperbolic reminiscence) that in the not-so-distant 'old days' children were sewn up for the winter in their woollen underwear, and unstitched only with the first warm days of spring. I have also heard similar stories about London evacuee children sent into rural areas during the Blitz (in their case not about the permanence of underwear but the total absence of it) – and, come to think of it, poor rural children could not have been that much better off themselves.

Luckily, they didn't all look like Oliver Twist before his supper. (Or after his supper, for that matter.) As I have said elsewhere in this memoir, plenty of parents worked hard enough, and showed enough self-respect and awareness of the priorities, to send their children to school not only well-behaved and well-dressed, but well-disposed towards the educational process. In other words, there were some smashing kids there too, and some smashing parents. And not all English either.

I had had no idea of what was going to hit me, but it seems I had arrived at the near-beginning of the great post-war immigration seepage into the cities of England. I say 'near-beginning' because the first signs had been the West Indian influx in the late forties. What I came across was the first billows of the Asian tide in the fifties. There had been a few varied dollops here and there in between – for instance, the arrival of Hungarian refugees after the abortive rising in Budapest in 1956. There was also an older scattering of Poles, Lithuanians, and the like, presumably the victims of the Second World War. But the Indians and Pakistanis were the ones who really got their teeth into it. Well, they did round our way up north.

To their credit, they were usually among the best behaved. Partly, I suspect, because they were, for a while, completely bemused by what was going on; they didn't speak a word of English. It seems hard to credit it now, in the age of counsellors and welfare officers and 'advisors' (which somehow sounds more important than the correct 'advisers'), not to mention the legions of 'relationships facilitators' and 'human resources managers' – all the serpentine ramifications and circumlocutory jargon of 'social services'; but, so far as I could make out, nobody was there to help these children at all. They just appeared in class, and had to get on with it – silent, blank, moon-faced, like little Martians.

Luckily for them, the playground provided all the social services most children needed – in company, advice, help, shoulders to cry on, worldly wisdom, local lingo, and gutter wit. Within weeks, they were capable, as one diminutive girl proved, of telling a tiresome bully to 'get lost'.

One factor in their favour was, surprisingly, arithmetic. Where they came from, they used Arabic numerals too. After all, a sum was a sum, and many of them soon began to knock spots off their home-grown classmates. It did wonders for their self-respect.

We had one Lithuanian lad of about ten or eleven, whose family had clearly been in England for quite a while, who was streets ahead of the whole class, in everything. Bright as a button. I discovered that the Lithuanian community in the city, like many minorities, was highly organised, and conducted lessons in Lithuanian for their children on Saturdays. So this boy would grow up enjoying a perfect ease of relationship with his contemporaries, while at the same time absorbing a deep understanding and appreciation of his national language and traditions. Food for thought there, I should say, for our social engineers.

Indians, Pakistanis (nobody had heard of Bangladesh in those days), Lithuanians, Poles, a scattering of West Indians, Arabs, Jews, Scots, and Irish – with names like Singh (of course), Patel (of course), Aaron, Hussain, de Courcy, Etienne, Ullah, Vymeris, Woloszczak. And that was just the surnames. How about these for Christian names? Can you imagine calling these kids in for their dinner? Bohdan, Kausar, Iswer, Liamutis, Loftus, Jethabet, Harbhajan. It was a feat to read the register, never mind teach them anything. This mixture may well be commonplace in many cities today; I am not a census administrator. But my impression is, and was, that it was only just beginning when I entered the profession.

As for what you might call the 'native' population, they couldn't have been more English and four-square and conformist and right-down-the-line. Traditional too

– names that you don't come across much now – Leonard, Ronald, Stanley, Donald, Herbert, Sydney, Norman, Albert, Arthur, Granville, Harold. Or perhaps this is a regional matter; perhaps they still have names like that in the outback beyond the Watford Gap. I wouldn't know. That's southerners for you.

But whatever the truth of the above, those older names were outnumbered by the rock-bottom favourites – John, Michael, Peter, Brian, Robert, Alan, Tony (or Anthony). Only one William, somewhat surprisingly, only one Paul, one Philip, one Thomas, one Christopher. But a whole rugby team of Davids. That was far and away the most popular.

With the girls it was Jean, closely followed by Christine and Patricia. Next came Margaret, Carol, and Barbara, followed by Ann and Kathleen. After that, in ones and twos – Brenda, Marie (only one Mary), Joyce, Hazel, Joan, June, Sandra, Maureen, and so on. Not many hothouse exotics – Vivienne, Camille, Noelle. And, as with the boys, some older favourites – Marion, Freda, Rita, Nancy, Irene, Muriel, Mavis, and Marjorie.

What is particularly noticeable in the light of modern society is the complete absence of the Shanes and the Waynes and the Traceys and the Sharons, never mind the Joleens and Terriannes and the Corralyns. (Now what caused that tidal wave of derivatives? Films? Affluence and consequent social aspiration? Television serials?)

How do I know all this? Or remember it? No trick, no feat. I have always been a hoarder of documents. I have lesson notes from pretty well every year I have taught. Class lists too. So there it was; all I had to do was blow off the dust.

What did I teach this maelstrom of mixed sex-age-race-nationality-social background? Probably not very much. What did it say on my timetable? I can answer that more easily – English, History, Scripture, Games, and, for one fraught term, Maths. I hadn't clapped eyes on a formula or a theorem or a logarithm since I was fifteen. So it would be more merciful to draw a veil over the Maths. Much later I did not have the face to include it in my CV. English, History, and Games – yes, I did know a bit about *them*, in a distant, academic sort of way. But Maths! God help us – and the children.

Of course the first lesson a teacher has to learn is not to collect information so much as to transmit it, and, to do that, he must first make it palatable, digestible – if there is such a word, learnable. So lofty acquaintance with Pitt the Younger's foreign policy and the economic rivalry between Rome and Carthage, or the subtleties of clause analysis and indirect speech, had to undergo some plastic surgery to be of any use in the classroom.

So I had to come down off my academic perch and think of ways to catch the interest of streetwise children whose view of life was bounded by terraced housing and the local football or rugby league ground. Luckily I had the wit to see that all that high-flown knowledge could be put to use if you sugared it up and doled it out in manageable doses. Luckily too I soon realised that, terraced housing or no terraced housing, they had more than their usual ration of shrewdness and native wit. If I could present legends and stories from the past in a way which treated the human condition in terms which they found relevant to their own lives, I could be in business. They understood greed, envy, sacrifice, ambition, pretence (they were especially good at spotting that), jealousy, fear, bravery – in short, all the usual human emotions.

So they could see the sense of solving the shortage of admirals faced by the Commonwealth by taking successful generals and putting them on the quarterdeck. They could appreciate the wiles of Delilah at work on the success-drunk Samson. They could understand what a colossal gamble it was for Duke William, in his small duchy, to take on one of the most important kingdoms in northern Europe; Hastings was anything but a foregone conclusion. They savoured the subtlety of Odysseus in having the chassis of the wooden horse trolley made deliberately wider than the gates of Troy, because he knew that the Trojans were incurably curious, and would do anything to get that horse inside their city and out of the clutches of the Greeks. So they pulled their gates off the hinges to get it in, leaving themselves wide open.

And I remembered one big lesson taught me by the Army: keep them busy. So we had lots of notes to copy from the board and lots of tests to learn for. Everything dedicated to keeping idle hands and the Devil at bay.

Was my work in line with the curriculum? I shouldn't think so. The only curriculum statement I saw related to the 'Accepted Syllabus' permitted in the Scripture lessons, for fear of offending other religious minorities (this was a church school). I was left with pretty much a free hand. Which meant that I could choose which part of the deep end to jump in from

Did I do any good? I shall never know. Did any pupil go on to take 'A' Level English or a degree course in History because of me? I very much doubt it. Whether I was any good or not, the dice of life were pretty loaded against most of them. About a half-dozen or so, in a good year, would pass the eleven-plus exam; the rest would stay on at the school till they were fifteen. So it would be terraces and football grounds once again.

Did I have disciplinary troubles? Of course I did. Some I handled better than others. I was well backed up by the deputy head, Jack Milford, and, when he arrived, by the new headmaster. And, oddly, by the occasional parent, in the most direct way. Not all mothers and fathers came steaming into the school loaded for bear, and looking for staff scalps. There was one gentleman, whose son, about eleven years old, was giving me a good deal of grief. He came in one day, as we were packing up to go home. He knew well that his boy had been in trouble, because of the various letters, notes, and general vibes reaching home. He came in armed with a shiny new cane. Coming straight to the point, he pressed it into my hand, and urged me to use it on his son's backside whenever I saw fit. Shortly afterwards, I did indeed see fit, and duly used it, in the recommended place. Our Victor rushed off, calling down fire and brimstone, but came back the next day as if nothing had happened, and I don't recall having any further trouble with him. Perhaps Dad had added a postscript when he got home.

It sounds like an echo from a distant era now, but we, the staff, were allowed to use the cane – with both sexes. (All right, only on the hand for girls.) Before the children's rights champions reach for their superlatives, let me point out that having the right to do something does not mean that one constantly exercised it. After all, the Queen has the right to dismiss the Prime Minister and dissolve Parliament, but she doesn't do it – well, not off her own bat. It's like those Hollywood films about the old-time Navy, none of which was complete without the indispensable flogging or keel-hauling. One would leave the cinema convinced that the British Navy was officered entirely by clones of Captain Bligh. Not so. In fact, modern research is showing that not even the press gang was as active as the legends, and Hollywood, would have us believe, never mind the cat.

It was the same with caning in schools. The wicked bamboo was not swishing about all the time. I remember caning only two children in my nine months there – our Victor, and one girl. (And believe me, a newcomer would remember inflicting a punishment like that.) Leslie never gave me any more trouble, and the girl, when the time came for her to leave, came to see me to say goodbye, and she was in tears at the prospect of leaving us all.

I had my successes and my failures, and my feuds. Perhaps the most difficult was a boy in the top class, who had long since grown out of his desk. He was due to leave at Christmas, so I was to have him only for about six weeks. He was well over six feet tall, with shoulders to match, built like a steel girder. I can't remember what precisely I did to cross our Francis, but cross him I did. He smouldered for the last two or three weeks, and in so doing passed on the sparks of his rage to his seedy lieutenant, whom we shall call Trevor. Trevor soon manufactured some grievance or other of his own. Some time during the final week of the term, they announced to anybody who happened to be listening, taking care to include me, that on my way home after breaking up they were going to get me.

Did I snap my fingers at them? No. Did I go to the

police and tell them of the threat of GBH? No. Did I tell Jack Milford? No, I don't think so. Did I slip a cosh into my brief case? No. Did I worry? Yes. So what did I do?

I waited for a good hour after all the children had gone. This was midwinter, remember, so it must have been getting dark. I fancied that, if our Francis and our Trevor were indeed waiting, they should have been pretty chilly and fed up by this time – might even be worrying that they had missed me. I slipped out of a back door, left by another road, and legged it for the bus station.

I never heard any more of Trevor. But I did hear that Francis had gone and got a job straight away in an Icelandic fishing fleet. At fifteen. Which gives some idea of how tough he was. So I was lucky, I reckon.

But they were the worst. As with society in general, most of the children, most of the time, were pretty law-abiding. Like most of us, they wanted a quiet life. They were, as often as not, prepared to give you the benefit of the doubt. If they saw that you were prepared to put your back into it, they would give it a go.

They were generally polite. On my very first day, the took me into their confidence with the news that after school they were going 'choompin''. I imagined that this was some local slang for a nefarious activity like pinching apples. But no – it meant collecting firewood for the Guy Fawkes bonfire (I started on November 5th, remember?) A few weeks later, I was asked if they could 'trim oop'. I glanced furtively at the back of their necks, to see if the barber was going to have much work to do. But, again, no – they were asking if they could put what were obviously traditional Christmas decorations round the classroom.

Some had remarkably adult qualities. One bespectacled little miss in the top primary class, about to take the eleven-plus, had boss's secretary written all over her. I would have loved to find out whether she actually did become one. Another really did perform some of a secretary's work; she was in fact the Head's PA. Before I had been at my desk two or three days, there was a firm knock on my door, and in came Alison Gordon. Neat. Brisk. Businesslike. With a bulging folio of papers and circulars and questionnaires clutched to her chest with both hands.

She couldn't have been more than ten or eleven years old. She was the boss's right-hand 'man'. There was no school secretary in our school. Obviously Alison could not take on the full responsibilities of a proper secretary, and she could not afford to miss too many lessons. In actual fact, she probably did what I am describing only two or three times a week, if that. But she made such an impression that one could be forgiven for crediting her with much more than she was actually doing.

I repeat, she may not have been entrusted with matters of high import, but what she did do she did with total confidence and aplomb. Within her range, she knew exactly what she was talking about. She knew exactly what had to be done, and she knew exactly what she wanted you to do.

And you found yourself doing it, without question. The visit went something like this.

'Good morning, Alison.'

'Good morning, sir.'

'What have I got to do?' (Even as early as this, I had learned the drill.)

This got her as far as your desk. Before you could think

of anything else to say, she went into her scenario. The first sheet was peeled off the top.

'There's this letter from the office that Mr. Milford wants you to read. . . . thank you, sir. And would you sign it here, sir, to say that you've seen it.'

She leaned slightly forward to check that you had. Another paper would be produced.

'There's this circular, sir. Mr. Milford says it's not very important. You only have to read these paragraphs – here – and here. That's right, sir.'

I almost waited for the comprehension test. A third document.

'Your expenses form, sir, which you sent in last week. You forgot to put your signature.'

'Oh. Sorry. Where do I – er – ?'

'Right there, sir.'

'Ah.'

And so it went on. She was infallible. She was a classic illustration of the adage that if you tell somebody to do something with enough confidence, they will do it. You knew she was only ten or eleven, but you found yourself relying on her totally. If Alison said it was so, it was so.

There were not many children there with Alison's gifts, but there were a great number with her solid character and equable temperament. They did not find life easy, but they accepted what could not be changed, and they had been inculcated by their parents with a generous ration of common sense, decency, and self-respect. You felt that, within their range and their type of society, they would make good citizens.

In the case of Alison and her potential secretary classmate, they were helped by having teachers like Cissie

Mannering. Cissie was in charge of the top primary class, the ones who were going to take the eleven-plus in the spring. Not many were going to make it, and Cissie knew that. But it was her job to try and bring them on as much as she could, to give them their best possible chance of breaking through to grammar school. At the same time, she had over twenty other children in the same room, to whom God had not been so generous with the little grey cells, but who equally deserved her attention, for different reasons.

She delivered on all counts. She was a grey sort of lady, whose age I did not dare then, and would not dare now, to estimate. But she was clearly very experienced, and this had given her the steadiness and reliability and, above all, consistency which children treasure. She did not patronise; she did not hector, she did not nag; she did not have favourites; she did not flap; she just got on with it. She did not pontificate in the staff room either, or gossip, or moan. If she criticised, she did it with a sort of dry, long-suffering tolerance that you may have associated with the old Jewish comedians. Like the children, I found myself respecting Cissie not for what she did, but for what she didn't do. The Cissie Mannerings of this world are among the jewels of the profession.

So I learnt a lot in my first six weeks. By the time we had 'trimmed oop' on the last day of the Christmas term, I was sensible enough to see that I had a great deal more to learn, but I could feel that at least I had made a start (as long as Francis and Trevor did not make mincemeat of me on the way to the bus station).

All that remains is to explain the title of this chapter.

We had another teacher, a young one, who taught Domestic Science (or Cookery or Home Economy or

Food and Nutrition – whatever you fancy). Pretty fresh out of training college, I should judge, or I judged then. Like all young teachers, she had to put up with kids trying it on. Well, it's part of the game, isn't it? If you can't try it on with the new teachers, who can you try it on with? The older boys were of course the worst offenders, which is no surprise either. The ringleader in his class was Bernard James, whose over-confidence grew with each, as he saw it, success.

Alas, he made the classic mistake of underestimating the opposition, and it was his undoing. He did not observe sufficiently sharply that Miss Cleaver was well built, with a fair circumference of upper arm. She had dark eyes, which could flash as easily and as ominously as a red traffic light. And she was Yorkshire born and bred, like him (so he should have known).

Anyway, one day, he was embarked on his, by now, usual campaign of Miss-baiting – fidgeting, nudging, smart answers, giggling – the usual things. They were gathered round a demonstration which Miss was giving by the stove. Then he must have ventured further than usual, getting ready to snigger to his mates.

Miss Cleaver stopped what she was doing, turned fully towards him, and fixed him with an incandescent eye.

'Are you mekkin' eyes at me, Bernard James?'

Bernard had gone too far to back down. His mates leaned forward expectantly. In for a penny, in for a pound.

'Yes, miss.'

There was a resounding 'thwack!' from a powerful right arm, and our Bernard had four livid red marks across his cheek.

He didn't do it again.

Ordeal in the lino department

EDUCATION IS A GREAT big con, isn't it? When you think about it.

There are twenty-five or thirty of them (sometimes more) and only one of you. You have no weapons of terror, and, as the twenty-first century advances, fewer and fewer sanctions of any kind whatever. The vast majority can think of a dozen places they would rather be than cooped up in a classroom with you, and the chances are that they are not exactly delirious about the subject either. And if they are not over-endowed with grey matter, they are nevertheless worldly enough to know that they are not going to scale academic heights. (Quite often the less academic they are, the more realistic are their assessments of themselves.)

So it has to be a con, doesn't it?

Now, of course, that is glib, and slanted, and deliberately so. Rather like some of Oscar Wilde's one-liners. But, like so many similarly slick verdicts, and like some of Oscar's *obiter dicta*, it contains a truth. (What is missing is the rest of the truth.)

However, let us take this particular 'truth' and, in order to measure the value of it, let us set it in a particular context.

The context is, or was when I was involved with it, a grammar school. I was teaching English. The class was about twenty-five to thirty thirteen-to-fourteen-year-old boys. And they were in the bottom third of their academic year. In the parlance of the time, they were 'C stream'. There were going to be no future Nobel prizewinners here. (The very word 'stream' dates it, doesn't it?)

So the example is pretty close to the 'rule' I stated at the outset. I was outnumbered at least 25-1. I never caned anybody. Not allowed to. I had only two sanctions – giving lines or putting them in detention (half an hour after school, so all they had to do was catch a later bus or train, and there was no shortage of those). They came regularly enough to school, because their parents had paid good fees for them to be there. But they were by no stretch of the imagination academic, and they knew it. And I never heard any C-stream boy of my acquaintance utter any sentiment to the effect that he couldn't wait to get to the next English lesson.

The only thing in my favour was that they were, by and large, sociable and willing souls; they were well-disposed to the human race; and they cheerily accepted the fact that for the next three or four years or so they would have to sit in tight, old, well-carved desks and be subjected to a series of lessons in subjects that, given the option, they would have been most unlikely to choose. That was life, they reckoned, and it was only from nine to four, five days a week, thirty-nine weeks a year, and fortunately life had its compensations.

So how was I going to make English tolerable and do-able?

It may be here that you would expect me to revel in pious and ponderous platitudes about spreading Culture, and the richness of words, and it's their own language, and the joys of poetry, and the glory of the Bard, and I don't know what. If you really think that, then quite clearly you have never stood in front of a classful of thirteen-year-old C-stream boys, five days a week, for thirty-nine weeks out of the fifty-two.

To help you understand why I was not going to attempt anything like that, you need to be told what it was that I was supposed to be getting across. What did 'English' in the timetable actually mean? And five times a week, remember.

English in the 1960's – at any rate in the grammar school where I taught, and my impression was that what we were doing was pretty universal – was a good deal more 'charged' than it is today. Take a look at this scheme of work, and compare it with what you did at school yourself. Or what your children are doing now. I don't say it was necessarily better – only that it was probably different. It is for the reader to cast his verdict.

In no particular order, we did punctuation – all the usual things – commas, full-stops, semi-colons, colons (colons – ever heard of those?), hyphens (and those?) apostrophes (for possession and omission, not plurals), dashes (what are they?), exclamation marks and question marks. We did spelling tests. We learned the parts of speech – I would be tempted to take a bet that a large portion of sixth-formers today would have trouble differentiating between a conjunction and a preposition, as evidenced by their constant use of 'like' instead of 'as'.

We had to recognise figures of speech – not only the eternal similes and metaphors, but rarefied phenomena like hyperbole and paradox.

We took sentences to pieces. We learned to recognise a finite verb and the four infinite parts of the verb. We became adept at spotting the difference between a clause and a phrase. We became acquainted with that hallmark of sloppy writing – the floating participle. Things like: 'Watching TV each evening, my homework never gets done.' (A concomitant curse of modern prose, visible daily in newspapers and media captions, is what one might call the wandering epithet. For example: 'The typical couch potato, overweight and unfit, any doctor would despair of him.')

We did precis and comprehension exercises. We read novels. We tackled the odd poem. And yes, we 'did' a Shakespeare play too.

True, we did not take any of these activities up to the level of what they did at GCE, or in the General Sixth I discussed in 'Second Time Around'. After all, they were thirteen, not fifteen or sixteen. Nevertheless, it was here, in the Third Form (Year 9 today), that the training began. By the end of the academic year, they could recognise a finite verb, a participle, a simile; they could summarise a simple piece of prose; they could tell the difference between Direct and Indirect Speech, and change the one to the other. In short, they had grappled with the English language.

So you have to be quite a con artist to get them to tackle all that, week after week.

Not only had they grappled with the language; they had composed it, created it. We did an essay every week. Friday lesson – set it. Friday homework – do it. Monday – collect it. Tuesday – mark it. Wednesday – return it and have a post-mortem.

Most people are not creative. It is as much as most of us want to do to put together a letter to the local health authority. Take Wodehouse's favourite character, Bertie Wooster. One of his typical efforts went like this:

'Dear Freddie,

Well, here I am in New York. It's not a bad place. I'm

not having a bad time. Everything's not bad. The cabarets aren't bad. Don't know when I shall be back. How's everybody? Cheerio!
Yours,
Bertie.
P.S. Seen old Ted lately?'

All right, so that's a bit over the top, and Bertie was a prize twit, but Wodehouse, like all good jesters, makes a valid point.

I think fear may have something to do with it. We know we can't write like Dickens or *Times* leading article journalists, so we conclude that anything which falls short is open to ridicule. Secondly, and at the risk of sounding precious, writing a piece of English prose is creative. It's called a 'composition', remember? You are composing something. Out of nothing. If you don't cheat and copy from somewhere else, it means that it has to come out of you. To a certain extent, therefore, it represents you. *It is you.* Therefore, in however humble and bumbling a way, you are laying yourself out on paper. You may not have to suffer the savaging of the literary critics in the surviving broadsheets and the long-haired journals, but you have to undergo a teacher's marking, which can be worse. One careless remark in red ink, or a thoughtless crack when handing back the homework, and a boy can clam up for weeks, maybe for the whole year. He's not going to lay bare his soul like that again, for you to tear to pieces. You have lost him.

Now add in to the formula the inexperience of a thirteen year old, the schoolboy's natural philistinism, and his very human preference for media entertainment or fresh air to prose composition. You now have a situation which will tax the ingenuity, resource, and sheer cunning of the teacher to the uttermost. How the devil do you get them to write something? Anything.

Despite what many may think – particularly the 'allow them to express themselves' school – it is no solution to give them freedom of choice. Take it from me, 'Write what you like' is the short cut to apathy, frustration, brevity, and mediocrity. Just as most of us are not creative, so most of us don't have much idea of what to do with total freedom.

There have to be rules, parameters, schemes, plans, aims. It is the difference between setting up a game of Association Football, complete with referee, on a properly-marked field, and allowing a free-for-all kick-about in the park. If you want to learn the piano properly, you have to get stuck into the scales and the arpeggios, under the eye of a teacher; you can't tinkle about on your own with *The Blue Bells of Scotland* for ever.

So a teacher must plan. And he must not only plan the individual essay; he must work out a scheme of types of essays, styles of writing, levels of complexity and sophistication. And he must get it across to the class what he is doing. They like a teacher to take off the lid and show them the works. It's part of the game – taking them into the club; people love being shown trade secrets. Boys – children, young people, indeed any group being taught – like to know where they are going. They like to get there. And they like to be able to look back and see where they have been. It is a very human desire, and the most philistine schoolboys are not immune to it.

So it becomes a joint venture. You may be the driver, but they become the crew. It is part of the trust-building exercise. If you are going to get them to accept your methods, your choices of essay subject, your marking, your remarks in the margin, and your criticisms, you have to take them into a sort of partnership. Not 'this is what you have to do', but 'this is what we are going to have a crack at' this week.

It is the purest common sense, of course, to start with something simple. Like the hurdling exercise I described in the chapter entitled 'Us don't 'ave no books, sir'. Get them to jump over a rope lying on the ground first, and then gradually build up to the height of the hurdle, indeed a height slightly *above* the hurdle.

What is the easiest form of writing? Straight narrative. Get them to tell a story. Not make it up. Just talk about something which had happened to them. Don't leave it there; you will get people who will find difficulty in doing even that, because they think that nothing interesting ever happens to them.

So you must prescribe it further. Get them to write about something you *know* has happened to them, and which has happened to nearly everybody. Say, 'The first time I told a lie' or 'My first visit to the dentist' or ' The first time I broke a school rule' – things like that. (Later on, when I was teaching girls, I could choose things like 'The first time I put on make-up'.) In the interests of humour, I slipped in 'My first cigarette'. We had a laugh almost at once. One boy looked distinctly worried, or at any rate pretended to. I asked him what was the matter.

He said, 'I can't remember back that far, sir.'

So we got off to a good start. But whatever they chose, they had something to go on. Their problem was not to wonder what to put in, but what to leave out. After all, we only wanted a page or two of an exercise book, handwritten. So length was not a worry; all they had to fret about now was technical accuracy.

That was the first step then. Showing them that, given the right preparation, there was no problem in covering a couple of pages.

They could now approach the next stage – writing a descriptive essay. Once again, prepare. What do you describe if you are giving a pen portrait of, say, a person you know? Question and answer round the class– physical appearance, naturally. Face, physique, dress, smartness (or not, as the case may be). Character, personality. Habits, mannerisms. Speech – accents, volume, level of correctness, favourite sayings. Strengths and weaknesses. Praise and criticism. Is that the full picture? What about anecdotes and stories to illustrate a particular feature? Always get stories in if you can; they are usually the most interesting. While all this is going on, build a list and lay-out on the board. After ten or fifteen minutes of this, you should have pretty well covered it – the board, I mean. You have made the point, visually, that, if they talk about every note you have made, their problem, once again, will be not one of inclusion, but of exclusion – not what to put it, but what to leave out – not desperate collection, but rigid selection. They begin to see that it is well within their scope. Part of the trust-building business again.

You can refine this. Tackle the business of bias. Write three short essays – one by a friend, one by an enemy, one (so far as is possible) with the truth. Or again, what about writing a pen portrait of yourself? Or doing word sketches of a teacher – by his pupils, his colleagues, his headmaster, an inspector? This can open up all sorts of byways about bias – how do you spot it? How do you do it? How do you avoid it? What are the tricks of the trade? Scope for another essay or two.

From there you can move on to what you might call the Expository Essay. In plainer English, explaining something. Thinking clearly. Working out the various stages in a particular procedure. Being logical. Putting yourself in the reader's position. Subjects? What about 'Building and lighting a fire'? 'Mending a puncture'? 'Taking a bike to pieces (and putting it together again)'? 'Making pastry'? 'Decorating'? There are scores.

The overall object, it should be clear by this time, is not to produce Great Writing, but to produce writing. Plain and simple – a couple of pages. Getting them to see, again, that it is well within their grasp. It becomes a job, like doing a bunch of equations or a batch of French exercises.

Now, if you think you have made some progress, why not take the same subjects, and get them to combine two techniques – describing the process, and at the same time producing a narrative about the terrible tangle you got into while attempting the process? If you are lucky, you are likely to get some little sparkles of humour. It will become clear that some of them have a genuine knack of writing something entertaining. What is more, they will have enjoyed doing it. We all like the prospect of doing something that might make somebody laugh. So you have by now generated willingness, perhaps even a touch of eagerness.

Hence – I repeat, if you are lucky – you will, when you come to mark the work, come across titbits which are worth passing on. They won't be good enough to have the whole essay read out. It is a rare pupil who can sustain that sort of pace for two whole pages. (We are talking about the 'C' stream, remember?) But there will be the odd remark or sentence, even paragraph. If it's funny, they will all get a laugh out of it, and it will be at nobody's expense. They will all see that 'progress has been made'. They are getting better. It is almost becoming worth the effort. Trust is being built further.

From then on, take your pick. Try a piece where they combine description, narrative, humour, and The Big Let-Down. Say, 'Nerves at going to the dentist, and then finding that you have nothing to have done'? Or 'Hearing a mysterious noise in the middle of the night, getting terrified, and then finding that it is only next-door's cat'? That sort of thing. Once again, their own experience. They will all be different. And plenty of scope for reading bits out loud when you have the post-mortem.

From then on, once you have developed some momentum, the scope is vast.

Give them a chance to develop powers of imagination. Appeal to what schoolboys love to do – talk themselves out of a sticky situation. So arrange a set of circumstances, and invite them to explain how they came to be found, say, late at night, in the gutter, dressed in dungarees, with a sack containing marbles, wood shavings, and a lump of cheese. Or invite them to explain how they sold Nelson's column to an American tourist. And stand by. All right, it won't be Royal Command Performance stuff, but they will have covered two pages, and it won't have been too much of a chore. And there will be, or there should be, plenty for everybody to have a chuckle at during the post-mortem.

If you think you can get away with it, try a more serious

one. Years ago, I was taken by the story of a railwayman who had to cross the line every day on his way to the signal box. One dark, very foggy morning, he was about to step across the track when he saw, at his feet, among the ballast, a freshly-cut rose. Naturally, he stooped to pick it up. As he did so, the London express roared past him. That rose saved his life, and he wore a rose in his button-hole every day thereafter. So – write an essay to explain how that rose came to be there.

Introduce them to the technique of building atmosphere. What do you do to create one? Talk about observation. Which of a set of details is the most telling? Discuss examples. Then get them to have a crack at describing a large room or a village hall on the morning after a party. Convey the feeling of the interior of a cinema disused for several months. What would the laboratory of a mad scientist be like?

Somewhere down the line you can embark on one of the most difficult forms of writing – the Reflective Essay. The scope is endless – anything from 'Trees' to 'Younger Brothers and Sisters' to 'Being Ill ' or 'Being Bored'.

This is where I think a mistake is made by inexperienced teachers who set a subject like 'Hedges' to a class and expect a two-page outpouring of fluency and wit. It won't work. A reflective essay is an extremely difficult form of writing to bring off. If you don't believe me, you try it. Get somebody to give you a title, and then sit down and try and knock out two pages which are not chock full of cliché and twaddle.

A thirteen-year-old has to be given practice at all sorts of other, easier types of writing before being inflicted with a reflective essay. It would be like teaching him woodwork by setting him a project to make a kitchen dresser instead of starting him off with a letter-rack or a book-end.

But give them practice, show them the different types of essay, build their confidence, give a hint or two about sideways thinking (there are all sorts of ways to make a point with words), and you can get a lot of surprises.

For instance, I remember one boy who had to write about being bored in a dentist's waiting room. He did the usual things about the silence, and the awful posters on the walls about tooth decay, and the years-old magazines. Then he put some dots. . . . Then he wrote (he actually wrote it out), 'Tum-tum – tiddle-iddle-om-pom-pom-pom'. I thought that was priceless. He had done the trick. He had conveyed boredom brilliantly.

Another essay I recall was about Being Ill. This sufferer had been given some ghastly medicine. And he wrote, 'It tasted HORRIBLE.' No font that I know of on a computer can do justice to it. So it has to be written out by hand. Again, it was a delightful piece of sideways thinking. It hit the nail smack on the head. He had got it across.

A third example also demonstrates what can happen as confidence grows. This boy's choice of title showed not only that he had grasped the nature of the topic, but that he had secured an overall view of it. It was not just a chore at which he had to slave for the minimum of time needed to get away with it. He had grasped the job by the scruff of the neck and he had clearly enjoyed doing it. The topic this time was 'Getting Lost'. He wasn't content with that for a title; he put instead 'Ordeal in the lino department'. Now that was good writing before he had begun his first sentence.

One could go on. If you explain and discuss – and if necessary write examples yourself – you can get them to understand, and be prepared to have a go at, things like Parody, which is quite mature stuff. Again, preparation is the key. So, have a session to collect all the clichés we know about, say, Scotsmen – clans, tartans, bonnets, kilts, dancing, claymores, cabers, plaids, porridge, meanness, 'och-aye the noo', and so on. Then write an essay about the 'typical Scot'. Offer alternatives like the 'typical American', the 'typical Frenchman', the 'typical pop star', 'the typical spy', and so on.

Another source of entertainment is playing with English spelling. Once again, prepare – what does a foreign accent sound like? Then – what does it look like *if spelt phonetically*? So 'Sir' in formal English may come out as 'Sorr' in Irish, and 'Surr' in Devonian. Once more, give them some examples. Then turn them loose on a piece in a foreign accent. German gives quite a lot scope, with z's all over the place. Does it make their English markedly better? Probably not. But they have had some fun doing it, and anything which takes the chore element out of composition must be a good thing, if only for one week.

Take this a stage further, and get them to write, say, a familiar fairy story in completely phonetic English. So they have to compose a logical sequence; they have to think about how words actually sound; and they can enjoy themselves making all sorts of outrageous spelling 'mistakes' and get marks for it. You can get gems like 'yoozhooallee'. Once more, maybe not good for literature, but good for morale.

If you give it some thought, there is no end to the types and variations and experiments you can try, once you have built a relationship. But this is only a memoir, not an English text-book.

Once you have built a working relationship, the post-mortem can be quite a fruitful exercise, and, if you are seen to be paying attention to their errors, and, more important, to their corrections, it is surprising how much effort they are prepared to put into it. Any sensible teacher will have learned very early on that children like having their work marked, and marked helpfully; they like getting their work back; and they like having it back on time.

For several years, the timetable was such that we didn't have an English lesson every single day; we missed out on Thursday and had a double lesson on Wednesday. If you paced it sensibly, you could get quite a lot of work out of them, and concentration. The first five minutes was taken up with marks, predictably. Then came ten minutes or so with reading out bits and snatches which were worth repeating. And they weren't all necessarily funny; they could by now appreciate 'good' writing as well as amusing stuff.

Then they got on with the corrections. There is a great deal of difference between mere indication of errors and creative marking. This took time – most of the rest of the session. But we always had a break between the first and the second lessons. If I forgot, someone always reminded me: 'Aren't we having a break today, sir?' That break was necessary. Most of us find more than half an hour's concentration quite enough. But give us a break and we are prepared to have another go. It is quite an achievement for a class of thirteen-year-olds to be prepared so spend so much time on such a humdrum activity.

Of course they liked the jokes and the howlers. Better

still, they now felt sure enough of you to be prepared to laugh at themselves, because they knew that they were all engaged on the same quest – to write better English – and we are all human and we all make mistakes.

I recall one exercise in which they had to compose a prospective house-buyer's advertisement, which he wanted to insert into the local paper. This one ended something like this: 'We are looking for a four-bedroomed detached house with central heating, bathroom, and a separate W.C. in the Weybridge area.' (Bit of a long way to go if you are taken short.) We all enjoyed that one, *including the perpetrator*.

Now – all of this may sound too cosy for words – I don't know. I had several 3C's over the years. Were they all angels? No, of course they weren't. Some of them were a pain in the neck (look at my chapter on Kimber). Did they all love it? I shouldn't think so.

But enough of what I have described took place for it to have become my abiding memory of that particular set of circumstances. And, at a reunion decades later, a mature gentleman took the trouble to walk across a crowded hall to thank me for teaching him to write. So we do ring the bell sometimes.

And it illustrates what I said about teaching being a bit of a con. You have to plan and you have to scheme and you have to anticipate them and out-think them. You have to be on top of them and you have to be ahead of them – if such a geographical feat is possible. I have said this elsewhere, but I'm going to say it again: you can't run a classroom like a democracy. It is not a salon, or a forum, or a debating chamber; it is an arena, which abides in a perpetual state of friendly undeclared war. You are not bringing them on; you are taking them on. You win some and you lose some.

Did any of them become journalists or novelists or playwrights or government report-writers? I doubt it. But, with a class like 3C, that was not the objective. If I had to summarise what the objective was, I guess I should say something like 'making them unafraid of a blank sheet of paper'.

One Monday morning, as I was collecting the weekend's essays, I asked one of them how he had got on with it.

'Oh, all right, sir. I managed to knock something out.'

I'll settle for that.

Taking a Net

THIS IS A GOOD example of a phrase that is immediately intelligible to anyone who is 'in the know', but could mean all sorts of things to an outsider. For the benefit of those outsiders, it is nothing to do with fishing, or petty larceny, or butterfly collection, or spoiling someone's tennis practice. It refers to cricket. More precisely, to cricket practice. This is conducted on a separate wicket, usually in some corner of the cricket field. It is surrounded by nets nearly ten feet high. These nets prevent the ball flying off in all directions when struck by the batsman receiving the coaching, and saves the need for having fielders out at various points to retrieve and return the ball.

Players take turns to bat – say, for ten minutes each, depending on how many people you have there, and how much time is available for the whole session. The rest congregate at the bowler's end, and take turns to bowl to the batsman. The teacher in charge may have just one net to supervise, or, if he has whole squad of a dozen to fifteen boys, two or three. The whole enterprise is casually referred to in the school cricket world, not as 'cricket practice' or 'cricket coaching' or even 'practice' or 'coaching'; simply as 'the nets'. Alternatively, a teacher may describe what he has to do in a practice session after school hours as 'taking a net'. *Voilà.*

So now you know. But, as with so many other occupations, there is a great deal more to it than meets the eye. Glance through the transparent pane of glass in the classroom door, and you could be forgiven for thinking that teaching consists of a teacher setting a task, then sitting at his desk marking while the class put their noses into their exercise books.

Cast a cursory eye over the hedge as you walk past – usually at a distance (people who are not interested or knowledgeable don't walk up to have a closer look) – and you'd think it was a pretty leisurely business of a small group of kids taking turns to toss a few casual balls at a boy batting at the other end. There doesn't seem to be any great sense of urgency. This is perhaps typical of every non-cricketer's impression of any cricket event – from test match to tea tent.

Well, come with me to that distant corner of the ground, away from the pavilion and the changing rooms and the precious central wicket, and let us see, from really close up, what is going on.

If school finishes at four o'clock, the session should be under way by four-thirty. At the school where I did most of my coaching, there was a bus ride between school and ground, so an earlier start was not possible.

Time would also be taken up with the issue of kit (one of cricket's shortcomings is the variety and voluminousness of the necessary equipment – bats, balls, stumps, gloves, and the ever-increasing range of protective gear), and with the changing of clothes. The local rules decreed that cricket flannels were *de rigueur*, even though it was only a practice session. You certainly needed special footwear, and the white shirt and trousers lent an air of purpose; they made the point that this was not a playground morning-break knockabout, but a serious practice for a school team. You were there to work and learn, not to play and to get into bad habits.

The teacher had to allocate which boys were to work in

which net, and in which order they were to take their turn at batting. Even this was not as stick-a-pin-in-the-paper as it sounds. You may have a very good reason, for instance, not to expose your tail-end batsmen to the battery of the team fast bowler. If two members regularly knocked sparks off each other and caused disturbance, the simple remedy was to put them in separate nets. It didn't cure it, but it helped.

Let us assume, for convenience of explanation, that there is only one net this evening. All right, you tell the first boy to get ready – to 'pad up'. While he is doing that, you also tell the team wicket-keeper to get himself ready too, because he will be an integral part of the fielding practice you will be taking later. He puts on pads and has his gloves ready. He goes twenty or thirty yards away and puts a single stump into the ground.

Your first batsman is at the crease and ready to do battle. Now, how are you going to treat the next ten minutes? Because that is normally about all he is going to get. If you have five or six in a net, one is batting, three or four are bowling, and the wicket-keeper is standing by. If everybody gets ten minutes at the wicket, that makes sixty. Allow some minutes for each change-over, for the changing of clothes, the issue and preparation of kit, the walk to the nets, and back, and the putting away of aforesaid kit, and changing back; and it is getting on for six o'clock. And these boys are only mid-teenagers; they have to get home; they have to eat; and they probably have a couple of hours of homework waiting for them. Their energy and strength are not limitless.

So, I repeat, what are you going to do with the next ten minutes? Just let him bat? Plenty of argument in favour of that. There is nothing worse than a coach who steps in after every single stroke the boy has played, and tells him at great length what he has done wrong. Even if he is right, it can be very wearing on the morale. It has to be a compromise; of course bad technical habits must be ironed out, or at least curbed, but at the same time he must be allowed simply to play; after all, that's why he likes the game. The more so if he is a tail-ender; in the normal run of things a tail-ender (the ones who go in numbers 9, 10, and 11) can't expect more than a few overs at the wicket in a match (if he gets in at all). So he treasures his ten minutes in the nets; it doesn't matter how many times he gets bowled – he still gets his ten minutes' batting, and he doesn't want to be constantly told how bad he is, and having it *proved* how bad he is.

What about your *bona fide* batsmen? What do you do with them? All sorts of things. Yes, you do correct them, but not, as I said, too much. You keep up their spirits, especially after they have just been bowled three times. You praise, you encourage, you jolly along. Even if you have just bowled him comprehensively with your famous off-cutter, you soften the blow by saying something like 'don't worry; that was rather a good ball'. And we all have a laugh.

If necessary, you might borrow the bat and demonstrate. A risky procedure, this. If you get it right, fine. If you don't, your own reputation suffers. There is nothing worse than attempting to display the perfect forward defensive stroke and getting bowled all over the place by one of the team's non-bowlers.

Or again, not knowing when to stop. I was once offering advice to a pretty competent performer about going down the wicket to despatch a slow bowler over the sight screens. I made the point that it is not a practice that should be indulged in very often, but that if you are going to do it, make a proper job of it. You know – in for a penny, in for a pound. With a full backlift and a full follow-through of the bat. 'Like this,' I said. I borrowed his bat, and instructed one of the bowlers to toss one up. Everything went perfectly – feet, head, hands, timing – and the ball duly went soaring up and over towards long-on.

Then I made my mistake; I attempted to demonstrate it again. It went wrong. I attempted to retrieve the situation by having another go. It got worse. I forget how many times I made a mess of it before common sense prevailed.

With your better batsmen, of course you watch out for bad habits. But some are so ingrained that you should realise, after a while, that you are never going to eradicate them. At any rate not without unstitching the boy's whole batting technique, and doing more damage than good. Again, it is compromise and balance.

We once had a gifted games player, who, as early as twelve years old, showed that, in the fullness of time, he would have 'First Eleven' written all over him. There was not a great deal, frankly, that we needed to teach him. He was a complete natural. All we had to do was point him in the right direction.

But there was one oddity. (I'm afraid this gets a bit technical, in order to make the point). The senior cricket master and I both noticed that when he held the bat ready to face the bowling, the face of the blade was somehow turned inwards towards his legs. Whereas the purists all decreed that the face of the bat should be turned much more to meet the oncoming ball – for a variety of very good reasons which I need not go into here.

Now this was a talented young performer, who could go very far in the game, so we thought. It was therefore incumbent upon us, his coaches, to provide him with the very best technique possible to enable him to reach his full potential. That meant getting him to turn his bat further towards the front. We explained all this to him, showing how important it was for him to be in the position to play strokes on both sides of the wicket. As it stood, his repertoire would be limited. He listened and understood, and, bless him, obeyed. Now he held the bat with the face of the blade turned up the wicket.

And he began to underperform. He was still scoring runs, but his timing was somehow 'off'. The ball was not leaving the bat at the expected angles. Something was wrong. I couldn't work out what it was. Neither could the senior cricket master, and he'd been doing it longer than I had been alive.

Then, one evening, for some reason I now forget, he and I were standing not at the bowler's end, where coaches normally placed themselves, but down at the batsman's end, outside the net. This enabled us to get right up close, and the net of course protected us from the ball.

And then we saw it. As the bowler ran up to deliver the ball, this boy shifted both his hands on the handle of the bat. The movement was only minimal; if we had remained at the bowler's end of the wicket, twenty yards away, we should never have seen it in an age. But this microscopic shift of grip sufficed to change the angle of the blade of the bat. He had no idea he was doing it;

he was concentrating on the bowler and the ball. It was instinctive and habitual; he couldn't *not* do it. But the result of course was that the angle of the bat was now made correct.

Before we had 'corrected' him, the blade faced inwards towards his legs. His tiny, unconscious twiddle of the handle brought the blade into the correct angle facing down the wicket. But because we had made him *start* like that, when the bowler ran up, his twiddle of the handle made the bat turn *outwards*. No wonder he wasn't timing it properly; no wonder the ball was flying off at the wrong angles.

So correction and perfection are not always the right way. Incidentally, I should have known this, because a similar thing had happened to me when I was at school. One Saturday, early in the season, I scored a very respectable fifty. Two days later, I fell into the hands of a friend of the cricket master. He, the friend, had a venerable record of MCC coaching, and a tie and sweater to match. He put me into a net, tossed up a few balls, and then pointed out that my hands were 'all wrong'. I had to put the right wrist 'further round'. What do you do? You are an obedient schoolboy who wants to learn and who is being told Gospel truth by an MCC coach. I turned my right wrist round.

For the next month or more I never got another decent score. I was dropped down the batting order. I was frustrated and miserable. In the end I said to myself 'Dammit' and put my wrist back where I had always felt comfortable. And I promptly started scoring runs again.

There is indeed a lot to think about when you are trying to teach batting.

Bowling, generally speaking, does not get as much attention. Well, not at school level. You have a net; you have five or six boys to train; the batsman must be kept occupied. As a rule there is not much opportunity for the bowlers to do much more than run up and bowl. Detailed training of a bowler needs more individual treatment.

Moreover, bowling technique is much more integrated than batting. You can isolate a single stroke in a batsman's repertoire and develop it by regular practice and repetition. With bowling, the run-up and delivery are so tightly co-ordinated that if you try to take the bowling action to pieces you run the risk of making it impossible to deliver the ball at all. The minute you think consciously about your bowling action, you can't do it. It is a highly-co-ordinated piece of muscular activity involving the whole body.

Is there nothing you can do to improve a boy's bowling then? Yes, there is; it is not all hopeless.

In no particular order: you can lengthen or shorten his run-up to the wicket, based on your experience, which is much wider than his; you can nag him to keep his bowling arm higher at the point of delivery; you can advise him to vary his approach to the wicket, so that the ball comes at the batsmen from slightly different angles. It may only be a matter of an inch or two, but that can get a ball past a bat which has not made allowance for that changed angle. You can offer hints on variety; don't bowl the same ball every time. Fast bowlers can work on disguising a slower one; medium-pacers can do the same; spin bowlers can put down the occasional ball that does not spin. It is often the harmless one that gets the wickets, because the batsmen are usually expecting something clever. The bowler's grip on the ball can vary, according to whether he is bowling an in-swinger, an out-swinger, a leg break, an off break, and so on. Keen boys like discussing these things. It is good if you can find time for at least some of this during the session.

Incidentally, with regard to spin, the grip affects the way the bowler delivers the ball. Without going into detail, delivering a leg-break and delivering an off-break do not look the same; fingers and wrists are doing different things. A batsman who can concentrate tightly enough can learn to spot what is coming.

I was making this point one evening. I was standing at the bowler's wicket and shaping my bowling arm and wrist as if I were going to bowl a leg-break.

'Now,' I said, to the batsman, 'if I hold my wrist like this, what am I bowling?'

'Tripe,' said a nameless voice from behind me.

You have to be on the *qui vive* too.

All this time the wicket-keeper is waiting. He has put on his gear, he has driven in his stump, he has collected two or three balls, and he is waiting.

So, in between doing what I have described with the batsmen and the bowlers, and keeping an eye on the clock for the change-over at the end of ten minutes, and having warned the next batsman to pad up, you must take time out away from the net, take a couple of boys with you – maybe more, depending on how you wish to organise your fielding practice – and get going.

You have long since drummed it into their heads that people do not pay a lot of attention to a team's batting or bowling (as a group, that is), but they do notice the standard of fielding. Good fielding is a sign, a measure, of a team's discipline, concentration, and general morale.

And good fielding doesn't just happen; it has to be worked at, like everything else.

Surely you just pick up the ball and chuck it in? No, you don't. There are ways – right ways and wrong ways – of crouching to stop a ball in the outfield; of crouching in the slips; of catching; of throwing; of aiming, and knowing where to aim. All this has to be taught, and practised. They must be made to appreciate that every single ball may come in their direction, at varying heights and speeds – often very awkward ones.

So – make them work. That is why it is usually better to work with only two or three at a time; they get more pressure, and have less time to sit back and switch off. Of course, your poor old wicket-keeper is at it the whole time, because every single time the ball is returned, it is aimed at him. Or rather aimed at a spot just above the stump he has driven into the ground. It doesn't always get there, and he has to be something of an acrobat to catch them all. Because they are human, and make mistakes, it often turns out that the ball comes straight at the coach instead, and he has to do the business – and he has no thick gloves. It isn't all lofty instruction and dignified progress.

Many coaches favour using a bat to hit the ball at the trainee fielders, presumably to give a fuller flavour of what it is like in a real match. I could never get on with this; I preferred throwing the ball myself. I could exert much greater control and precision.

I could do the slow roll towards him; the fast roll; the oblique roll, so that he not only had to come in, but move sideways as well, and use extra judgment accordingly. I could vary the speed with much more finesse, and work up to quite difficult stuff. They can progress with fewer nerves if they move up the difficulty scale gradually, and it improves their confidence. So, after quite a short time, I could test them with the real pigs – the awkward ones that they could not reach before they hit the ground and could not get back from to take the bounce at the top of the parabola. They are absolute swines. With a throw, I could control these. With a bat, I couldn't. Precision meant success (for me); success meant higher frequency; higher frequency meant better performance, and better morale (for them).

Nobody, at first, likes fielding. It is a bit like practising scales on the piano. It is looked on as a chore. So work, pressure, is the great secret. Keep them too busy to get bored. And if they are there in twos and threes, none of them wants to under-perform in front of their team-mates.

As with their batting and bowling, you must keep up a flow of encouragement, praise, chivvying, lively comment. You can even be rude to them – so long as you have won their confidence, and they know what you are trying to achieve.

You keep your wits about you too, as I said. Seize on any chance to make a point.

I was demonstrating one evening, at the start of a fielding session, the importance of throwing the ball to the wicket-keeper's gloves just above the wicket. 'Throw to the top of the wicket' is the mantra. In order to make this point a little more theatrically, I placed a single bail in the groove at the top of the single stump, and we all stood back about twenty or thirty yards. I picked up a ball.

'Now,' I said, 'the perfect throw-in would dislodge that bail without hitting the stump.'

And I let fly.

The ball did exactly that. The stump never quivered.

I turned away.

'Like that,' I said casually, and moved on to begin the session.

There was a gasp of amazement. For once the gods were on my side, and nothing tempted me to try and repeat it. Wits, you see. Low cunning. Invaluable.

Now, I must ask you to remember that, while all this fielding is going on, the batting and bowling is continuing, but of course without the same level of concentration that would exist when the coach is in the net. A coach's eyes must be constantly cast in that direction, and the necessary exhortation to put a sock in it or to stop playing idiots must be administered.

Is that it then?

No – not quite.

You must find time to teach the captain how to be a captain. Surely that is just a matter of knowing when to change the bowling. Again, not quite. Yes, a captain does have to learn which bowlers to use, and when to change them. But he also has things to learn about setting a field, about directing fielders to where you want them to go – and making it look simple and casual. No fuss – that is the target – and, like everything else, it does not simply happen. It has to be taught, and practised.

He has to learn to be responsible for checking the team members are aware of the fact that they are in the side. He has to check that they are physically there on the day. He has to learn the protocol of meeting the opposing captain, and the opposing master in charge, of being the host team at tea-time, of thanking the tea-ladies, of making sure that the team's kit is safely, and completely, and neatly, stowed away at the end of the game. So many things.

There are the arcane mysteries of the myriad factors which influence a decision whether to choose to bat or bowl – assuming you have won the toss. A captain will naturally look to the coach to help him on this, but a good coach will have done the coaching well before the match starts. He has appointed the captain; he has trained him; the least he can do is to let the boy have his head. It is a great temptation to lesser coaches (those who wish to win at almost any cost) to make the decision for him. It is not unknown for a coach even to decide on all the bowling changes. The captain will feel inadequate and will learn less. His morale will be far higher if he feels that the coach trusts him to make a decision, and will back him if the decision proves to be the wrong one.

How do you fit all this into 'a net'? Probably you don't; you have to snatch a minute or two as you walk back from the nets to the changing rooms, or as the gear is being put away.

I have no doubt that many fellow-practitioners could put pen to paper to point out several vital points that I have missed. And I have no doubt either that they are right. But all I am concerned with in this chapter is to make the point that 'taking a net' is not all it seems from a casual glance. Even if my list of a coach's duties and responsibilities is not exhaustive, it should serve, I hope, to drive my point home.

I would, however, add one more item – the small matter of team-building. No team is a random collection of eleven individuals, however gifted they may be. If you have done your job properly, the team personality should end by being more than that of eleven combined individual personalities.

How you achieve this is a very personal thing. No two coaches go about it the same way. But I venture to suggest that most of them will, at some time, pay attention to some at least of the following factors.

Ideally, each member of that team should be made to feel that he has a role to play. He is not there just to make up the numbers – you know, batting number ten, never bowling, and long-stop at both ends. No matter how much you criticise and chase and nag, you must also get it across that you are on their side, and that their success means something to you. For their sake, not for the sake of your own record in the promotion stakes.

Don't butter them up too much when they win; don't kick them when they're down. Don't be a know-all. Be ready to admit your mistakes, because you are certainly going to make some. Insist on courtesy, on smartness, on punctuality, on correct manners both on and off the field. Make it clear that, while you appreciate their nerves, and understand their mistakes, and make allowances for their inexperience, you are also looking for the best possible team; if a member isn't up to it, he has to make way for somebody else.

There will be times when you have to stick your own neck right out. One final anecdote to illustrate this.

I usually coached the Under-15 team. So I inherited the group which had been the Under-14's the previous year. This particular lot had had a terrible Under-14 season. I don't think they won a single match. The *nadir* was reached when a rival school shot them out for seven. That's the whole team – all eleven of them – all out for seven. For all I know extras were top scorer. And they had batted first. The other team went in, knocked off the necessary eight, and the game was over before three o'clock. They were right down in the dumps.

It didn't help much at the beginning of the following season that water had passed under the bridge and that memories had softened. They knew that they would have to face the same boys in the same schools, who had progressed to the Under-15 teams just as they had. It didn't bode well.

The most obvious tactic was caution. And not to raise the hopes more than was practical. I forget now which way the early results went. Certainly they did not set the Thames on fire. But at least we had some full games. We achieved this by sending the opponents in to bat first whenever we won the toss. My captain was an intelligent lad, and could readily see the sense of this.

But the nets slowly began to look more promising, and our batting results began to show something approaching respectability. Confidence was beginning to seep back. I daresay that sheer time was also a contributory factor; they were simply getting older and stronger.

About half-way through the term, the captain and I were discussing the game scheduled for the coming Saturday. The weather was steadily dry and warm; our batsmen had had some satisfactory practice; our two openers were shaping up nicely.

It was scarcely surprising, then, when the captain said to me, meaningly, 'Sir, what do you think we should do if we win the toss? Put them in again?' That's what his words said; his face and manner said, 'Sir, we're cheesed off with playing it careful; we'd like to bat first. We'd like to chance our arm and see what we can do.'

The very fact that he 'said' this was a good sign; they were not the crushed rabbits of last year. They really felt they were in with a chance, and they wanted to be allowed to take that chance.

This was a classic example of the importance of timing. If I had said 'no', they would have obeyed, but they would have felt let down; they would have felt that I didn't think they could do it.

I had no idea whether they could or not. But they had worked hard; they had improved; they had looked forward to doing what other teams would do if they won the toss on a good, dry wicket – bat. I don't think they realised as clearly as I did that, if they came unstuck, and got shot out for next to nothing, it would put them right back again to last year. But they had to be given the chance. I did go so far as to say to the captain something like 'I presume you realise that this could be all or bust?' He said yes. He was a good captain.

They won the toss, they batted, and they put on over fifty for the first wicket. And they never looked back. One boy scored over 70 in one later match, and 100 in another. They finished with a very respectable record.

But that was the moment. That was the hinge. And, like the Battle of Hastings, it could so easily have gone the other way. If it had, it wouldn't have been their fault; it would have been mine. Had I thrown them in the deep end before they were ready? Or at least agreed that they should jump in the deep end? I was just lucky. But I have been grateful that I did not have to endure many more Friday evenings like that one, just before the match, wondering whether I had done the right thing.

That is what is involved with 'taking a net'. Next time you go past, have a closer look.

It takes the breath away

IF YOU SPEND A serious amount of time in almost any occupation, and keep your eyes and ears open, you will come across examples of ignorance, bad practice, idiocy, outrageousness, and sheer incredibilia (if there is such a word – and if there isn't, there ought to be).

Look at the history of the British Army: boys of twelve obtaining commissions; consignments of boots sent to the Crimea with no right feet – all left; Florence Nightingale discovering that the water from the main supply for the military hospital ran through the body of a dead horse; and of course the stellar shambles of the Charge of the Light Brigade.

Try the world of government bumf: during National Service, a group of us spent two days going through training pamphlets, crossing out 'jeeps' and substituting 'quarter-ton trucks'.

In the firmament of the arts, you can't move for lunacy: the piano recital that was given with the hammers removed from the keys, so that not a sound was heard – and somebody called it a major breakthrough; the completely blank canvas, with a tiny tear in the top left-hand corner, that was solemnly hung in the Royal Academy; the horizontal filing cabinet at an exhibition that my son and I sat upon because we were tired and desperate, only to be frostily informed that it was an exhibit.

Anybody can fill countless pages – if he is so disposed – with similar examples.

It will come as no surprise, therefore, to be told that the world of education is just as crammed full of such phenomena. Any other teacher with a few years' experience could offer just as many examples as I am about to present – quite possibly better ones. It's just that I happen to be the one sitting at a keyboard, and I am the one writing the book. And these are the things that happened to me. These are the things that I have been trying to get out of my system for years. Well, now I'm going to.

Where to start? It doesn't matter really. Let's begin with words; that's what we use all the time to express what we hope we mean.

You would think, wouldn't you, that the world of education, above all others, would set store by clarity, precision, economy, simplicity. After all, they are supposed to spend a great deal of time teaching children to express themselves clearly, simply, and fluently, so at the very least you would expect those in charge of the education process to set some kind of example. Well, stand by.

Take the business of nomenclature. What do you call things? The commonsense answer would be to give them names which reflect their situation, their function, their rank in the overall scheme. Not so in education. For instance, when the Great Comprehensive Crusade was unleashed on an unsuspecting nation, we were told that children were no longer to be 'labelled'. It sounded wonderful. What it meant in practice was just another set of names.

Now of course, if some imagination is shown, that could bring about an improvement. And this did sometimes happen. For instance, it made more positive sense to call children with poor eyesight 'partially sighted' than to continue to call them 'partially blind'.

But there didn't seem to be much imagination shown

when it came to christening classes, despite the authorities' frequent assurances that they were not going to 'label' children.

So what did they do? Instead of playing down the business of labelling, they put it in the middle and painted it red. You shouldn't, they said, continue to refer to three classes in the same year as the 'A' stream, the 'B' stream, and the 'C' stream. It would upset children because 'C' came lower in the alphabet, so the name would brand them as third-class citizens, with all the concomitant complexes which would remorselessly follow. So you changed the names, say, to 'X', 'Y', and 'Z'. Even that was not good enough camouflage; you reversed the order, so that the top stream became 'Z', the middle stayed 'Y', and bottom became 'X'. Who on earth did 'they' think they were fooling?

Any child, in any stream, from 'A' to 'Z', knew that one of those streams was bright, the second was average, and the third was – well, a bit slow, to say the least. Dammit, children are the greatest realists in the business. When one school I worked in instituted a system of merit cards to be awarded for good work, it was indeed welcomed, and the children were delighted to receive them, but 'Merit Cards' were very soon christened 'Creep Cards'. This does not show that the children were cynical or uninterested, but it did show that they had a healthily critical attitude to any educational do-goodery; they had a shrewd sense of perspective. They knew what was going on. And there is nothing wrong with that. After all, we have a slang word for medals – 'gongs'. That does not mean that we wish to abolish the awarding of them.

Faced with these problems, the reformers then decided

that, in order to get round this business of streams, by whatever name, they would abolish streaming. Have mixed ability. The comprehensive where I worked for sixteen years had a seven-form intake, and they were all mixed ability – except one. That was to be a remedial class, the place where pupils were put who needed special tuition tailored to their limited abilities. Very praiseworthy, and much needed, and the teachers in this class were dedicated specialists who did fine work. But what was it but a stream? Admittedly, only one, and a very slow one, but it was, to all intents and purposes, a stream.

But there the logic stopped. Just because you tailored a class for the children of least ability, you couldn't tailor a class for those of greatest ability. That was 'elitist'; that would give complexes to everybody else.

However, by the end of the first year in secondary school, it was becoming clear that you could not continue with mixed ability right across the board. With subjects like History and Geography and Art, maybe. With English, well, at a pinch. But with things like Maths and French, it was not workable. Widely varied rates of progress were making the teacher's job nearly impossible. I know of one colleague, a seasoned, highly-qualified, mightily conscientious teacher of French, who, in her attempts to keep occupied and motivated a mixed ability class (which included near-illiterates who hated school, and were backed up in every contretemps by their parents), drove herself to the edge of sanity, and was forced to take early retirement on health grounds.

The school management decided to remedy things in the second year by admitting that about one third of the pupils were above average, another third were about average, and the last were below average. (Real rocket science, this. I hope you are still with me.) So they split them accordingly. But they must not be 'labelled' 'streams'. No, no. They were to be called 'bands'. . . . Yes, I know – you tell me. And everybody continued to refer to 'top bands' and 'middle bands' and 'lower bands' just as they had referred to the old streams, with no discriminatory intent – purely as a simple means of reference.

But there was still to be no emphasis laid on 'coming top' or 'slipping to bottom'. On the other hand, it was blindingly obvious that the selection process at the end of the first year was not going to be infallible, and some mistakes would have to be remedied. Similarly, some children would work hard, improve, and deserve to be moved to a higher band. Or, if they were not up to it, to a lower band. We had meetings at the end of each term to decide these moves. But they were not to be called 'promotions' or 'demotions', not matter how obvious they were to all concerned, especially the children. No – these gatherings were to be known as 're-allocation' meetings. All moves were to be sideways. A spade in future was to be called anything but a spade. If it were to be a means of reassuring or encouraging children, one could perhaps accept it, but the system fooled nobody, least of all the children, who, I should have thought, would have lowered their respect for the whole business. It was a bit like the emperor's new clothes.

I was once invited to meet a county adviser or research officer or somebody or other, who had come to the school to collect some information on how well the whole concept of mixed ability was actually working out in practice.

To my shame, I found myself, in response to her

questions, mouthing the accepted platitudes about the avoidance of labelling, and an even chance to everybody, and the democratic principle, and the end of elitism, and similar cliché-peddling. I don't know why one does these things. Partly, I suspect, out of some kind of misguided respect for the poor person who has to gather such information. After all, you feel, they are only doing their job, and it is not for you to make life more difficult for them than it need be.

Then, thank God, I actually caught myself saying this stuff; I could hear myself speaking, as it were. I suddenly stopped, and said, 'Stop writing.' She had been scribbling away, filling in all sorts of squares and oblongs.

She looked up in surprise.

'Forget all that,' I said.

She blinked. I spelt it out.

'I don't believe any of that. I don't believe in the value of mixed ability as a general principle of education, and that's all there is to it.'

To her credit, she rose to the challenge.

'Then tell me what you do think.'

So I did. And she scribbled away even faster.

When I had discharged both barrels, I finished by apologising for ruining this particular episode of her research project. She put down her pen, and said with commendable martyred nobility, 'Not at all, Mr. Coates. What you have said is most interesting.'

I thought, yes, and a pig's ear. But she did surprise me with what she came out with next.

'Would you be willing to come to a meeting we shall be having next month? It will be a divisional gathering about Mixed Ability across several counties.'

'Why?' I said. 'I shall disagree with it. I shall be no use at all.'

'Oh, no,' she maintained. 'We should very much like to have views from the opposite camp. It will be most stimulating.'

Stimulating for whom, I thought. It seemed unlikely that a committee of reformers, assembled specially to discuss the ramifications and benefits of their cherished reform, would be agog to hear the opinions of a solitary dissident. He will not able to convince a regiment of radicals that they are wrong from the word go. No mere Moslem would have persuaded the crusaders that Islam was right. It seemed equally unlikely that that dissident would enjoy his role of echo from the past among a phalanx of modernists.

What I was being asked to do was to go a hundred miles, at my own expense, to be the chopping block for a conclave of eager educationists who were totally convinced of their own rectitude, and who would have relished the chance to denigrate and pour scorn on some nineteenth-century reactionary who would have finished the meeting as the shocking example.

So I didn't do myself much good there. The irony is, among other things, that it is difficult, I understand, to find many advocates of mixed ability now. It's a bit like trying to find a Nazi just after the War. Look at the debate over exams and coursework. Coursework was introduced in order to ease the pressure of exam nerves on worried candidates. Now, it seems, we are hearing more about reverting to one-off exams, a noble cause no doubt advocated by prophets as earnest as their 'coursework' predecessors. Stand still long enough in education, and the world comes right round to you again.

For instance, about thirty or forty years ago, a new gospel assured us that the way forward (they love the word 'forward', and they love sticking the word 'backward' to any opponent), with children in their first year at secondary school, was to deal with them not one class at a time, but two. So, if you had two groups in say, History, you taught them separately for one of the two periods, and for the second you had them together, in one big room. I won't go into the great merits that this new system guaranteed – so far ahead of what had gone before, you understand – because that is not my point. My point is that, when someone 'came round' to explain, from wherever it is that these people come round *from*, a seasoned teacher beside me grunted in disdain several times while this was being done. When I asked him why, he said, 'We were doing this thirty years ago.'

Then there was the business of the geography of the classroom. How many times have you been into a classroom, particularly a primary classroom, and seen small tables scattered in odd patterns, and the children sitting round them on every side, so that only a third of them can see the board? Another third have to twist their bodies. The last third don't see the board at all.

But then perhaps the teachers don't do much with a board, to warrant a whole class looking at it. Perhaps there isn't a board at all, so there's nothing for them to look at. No focus. Nothing to trap attention. Or is it all done by videos and DVD's? I have often been tempted by the thought that, one day, a young pioneer is going to shoot up the promotion ladder by saying, 'Look – why doesn't somebody put all the desks facing to the front, make the children all sit behind them, have a board of some of kind or other, and have the teacher standing in front of it explaining something and making sure they listen by constantly asking questions?' So long as he caught the attention of some county primary adviser who had nothing much on his plate at that moment, and wrote some articles in a left-wing journal, he could be a professor of education in no time.

No, maybe not, but I enjoyed flying the kite. Nevertheless, think for a moment how often you hear the complaint that children can not concentrate. How often do you feel frustrated yourself when you get the impression that so many television programmes are constructed for a viewing audience whose concentration span is estimated at about ninety seconds? Is that because the makers of programmes have decided that the damage done to children's powers of concentration has now seeped into the adult world – permanently and irremediably – or is it because the makers of programmes *themselves* have graduated from primary school with a permanently impaired concentration span?

Now, let us assume for a moment you can not manage to concentrate any more on children's powers of concentration, and move to something else – jargon.

Every walk of life has it. Newspapers do not report an investigation; it is a 'probe'. As the veteran broadcaster Alistair Cooke once remarked, a rocket sent out to have a look at the moon was given the headline 'Lunar Probe', as if, said Cooke, it was some kind of surgical procedure to combat advanced cretinism.

Civil aircraft are strewn with them. Passengers are now 'customers' or 'clients'. You don't ask for things; you 'request' them. You don't buy things; you 'purchase' them. You don't even purchase 'things'; you purchase 'commodities'. And so on.

The American army came out with some gems. How about 'collateral damage' for 'civilian casualties'? Or 'permanently impaired combat personnel' for 'dead soldiers'?

This isn't just me sounding off. Give anybody a drink, and give him the floor at the same time, and you can stand by for a broadside on jargon.

Well, the world of education is just as knee-deep in it as anywhere else. We have already met the 're-allocation meeting' for promotions and demotions. How about this one?

Admittedly I got this second-hand from a colleague who just been on a course (there's another hobby-horse waiting to be ridden). He said he had met a teacher who could barely open his mouth without coming out with this near-gibberish. Let us call him, for convenience's sake, Mr. Fadfollow. My colleague had just been talking about the surprising skills some pupils demonstrated that had little to do with the actual lesson in progress. Fadfollow asked him to give an example – or rather to 'personalise his experience'.

Well, said my colleague, he had discovered that one particular boy was very good at producing neat little diagrams to illustrate certain technical points, almost cartoons if you like. 'He was a better draughtsman than I am. So I asked him to do a set of drawings for me to help with a new project I was preparing. He was very willing, he enjoyed it, and the lessons went much better because of it.'

Fadfollow nodded sagely, as if he were well acquainted with the phenomenon.

'Ah, yes – child-orientated resources.'

My colleague spread his hands.

'The kid did the drawings!'

But you see the potential, don't you? Fadfollow could build a whole Ph.D. thesis on that. And swarms of advisers would invade schools county by county and urge 'child-orientated resources' to staff-rooms full of silent, dead-pan teachers looking at the emperor again.

I once had an adviser come to visit me taking a History class – about fourteen years old, I suppose (the class, not the adviser). They were just embarking on the start of their (then) 'O' Level course. As it happened, I knew him; I had met him at some conference or other. We were comfortable with Christian names. He was an amiable chap. I think his official title was Adviser in Curriculum Resources. Anyway, there he was, sitting beside me while I took this lesson.

At the end of it, it was morning break, so we had time to discuss things before the next class trooped in.

He pointed to some cupboards which lined the back wall.

'Why do you have those there?'

Hiding my surprise, I said, 'I keep our text-books there.'

He did not hide his surprise.

'But why don't you keep them in your book store?'

'Because I don't have one.'

'Ah.'

He tried again.

'I notice that you don't have much in the way of visual

aids up on the walls – calendars, time charts, pictures – that sort of thing.'

I pointed to the rest of the room. One side consisted of half-glass doors and windows giving on to a corridor. Opposite there were more windows and glass doors giving on to a playground. Behind us was a broad blackboard. And of course a whole line of rickety book cupboards at the back.

'Where do you suggest I put them?'

He looked disappointed, and came in on another tack.

'That's a pity. I envisaged a practical centre at the back of the room.'

I blinked.

'A practical centre?'

He waved vaguely.

'Yes. You know – work surfaces and sinks and taps and so on – making models and . . . . ' He waved vaguely again.

I said, 'These pupils are upwards of twelve years old. We work towards public examinations. We don't do papier-maché and sticky-back plastic.'

'Ah.'

I decided to take the initiative.

'May I ask you a question, John?'

He gestured expansively.

'Sure. Go ahead.'

This was going to be a bit sensitive, but I had started, as the man said, so I decided to finish.

'Please forgive me asking, but what exactly are your credentials for what you are doing?'

He smiled.

'Absolutely none. I have never taught a History lesson in my life.'

It was in my History room – where I met this tap and papier-maché man – that I was asked a similar question, though in rather different circumstances.

We were in the middle of a full inspection – HMI's (as they were known in those days: much more impressive, don't you think – 'Her Majesty's Inspectors'). As Head of History, I could expect to receive a visit from at least one of them. So I duly prepared. I thought the best thing to do was to show the visitor the sort of thing I did as a matter of routine. No dressed-up, smarmed-up showpiece which was going to fool nobody. The class in question – second-year, about thirteen – was due for an oral test, so I decided to go ahead with it.

What I usually did was to give out the necessary paper (no text-books or exercise books to be on view), ask the questions (repeat them if necessary), and then ask them to exchange answer papers. Total silence was expected while this was going on.

I read out the answers, offered the possible variations, and listened to queries about alternative answers which might be viable. I would go into Olympian mode, and decree what marks, or fractions of marks, were to be awarded for near-misses. Then they totalled the marks, signed the answer, and returned them. Now and again, somebody would query the arithmetic, and that would be that. I would take in the marks and record them.

It was routine. They had done it a dozen times. They played ball, and kept quiet when I asked for it. Now and then there might be a chuckle or two over a funny answer. And we always got through in the thirty-five minutes with just a minute or two to spare. If you like, the whole class was being professional and doing a professional job. They took no notice of the inspector after I had introduced her and explained the nature of her visit. She sat in her tweeds and cloak (cloak!) at the back, and they promptly forgot about her.

Because of her visit, and because I knew she would want to discuss the lesson at the end, I made a particular effort to move things just a little more quickly, so that we would have some time at the end before the bell went. When the marks were in, I explained that they would have to wait five or six minutes while I discussed things with the visitor, and would they please sit tight till the official end of the lesson. They did.

Of course, being children, they nattered a bit. But why not? They had just been in total concentration for nearly half an hour, and they had done a good job. But they were not rowdy or throwing things about. They were just sitting and chatting.

The inspector, however, did not seem to like this. Two or three times during our conversation at the back, she lifted her head and surveyed the class as if to say, 'You're letting them get a bit restive, aren't you? Shouldn't they be engaged in something fruitful?' She seemed to have little grasp of what had just been going on, or to appreciate that I had deliberately ended early for her sake.

But that wasn't the only surprise.

After the children had left, she turned to me and said, 'Just what are your qualifications, Mr. Coates?'

So I told her – after I had got over the shock.

Why the shock?

I'll be honest – it threw me for a minute. It was the last question I had expected. So if she had set out to destabilise me, she succeeded. But why would an inspector want to do that?

And think for a minute. Inspectors are supposed to be prepared. The headmaster supplies them with details of their staff – age, degrees, diplomas, schools taught in, position in present school, and general experience. Weeks ahead. She must have known. She came all that way down from London just to ask me that? Perhaps because of the shock, I have no recollection of what else was said – if anything.

It made one wonder just what sort of answer she had expected. Was I supposed to supply details of dozens of courses I had attended? Mysteriously, as we plied our trade, it was made clear to us by some kind of psychological osmosis that, if one wanted promotion, one had to go on courses. Interviewing bodies, we were assured, loved hearing details of the courses you had been accepted for.

I don't think it mattered much what they were. You just had to go on them. I remembered one I went to at the university nearest to us. It was for History teachers. As it was at the university, I made sure I gave a good impression – collar and tie, suit, polished shoes, the usual things. I sharpened my wits too, to prepare for the intellectual cut and thrust that we would be exposed to in lecture and discussion.

The lecturer, when he turned up, was in corduroy trousers, plimsoles, and open-necked, rather scruffy rugby shirt, and I remember his speech was strewn with colloquialisms and jargon. 'Well – great!' is one phrase which sticks in the memory. I had a music colleague who told me that she gave up going to courses because she got fed up with listening to speakers who were less qualified and less experienced than she was.

Time and again we wondered where these institute of education and training college lecturers came from, and how they had got their jobs.

One day I was in conversation with a colleague about our respective training. I had not done the fourth year after the degree – the one in which you study for the post-graduate certificate of education. That was because I had had no intention at the time of becoming a teacher. After I had entered the profession, I later took the certificate exams externally from London University. This lady had done the usual two years after leaving school at a teacher training college. We got on to the subject of the theory that was taught at such colleges, and I was chipping in with my two-penn'orth about the high-flown stuff I had had to read in preparation for the external exams.

She said to me, 'You know what? Not a single one of my lecturers at college had done any teaching in an ordinary classroom. Not one.'

I wonder what the moral is to that.

Or this:

As I said, after I had been teaching five or six years, I decided to study for the post-graduate certificate of education. It would make my CV look more professional, obviously. More earthily, it would mean more money. At the time – the early sixties – that came to about fifty pounds a year. Fifty pounds! Such was the value of money then. Nowadays it would buy you a West End stalls ticket or get half the family into Alton Towers for one visit. Ah, well.

I set about the reading list necessary to obtain some

kind of mastery of the topics to be examined – educational psychology, the English educational system, the history of education, the philosophy of education, and so on. I obtained some past papers, and did some trial essays by myself. In fact, when I set some of my sixth forms history essay tests, they had no idea that Sir, up at his desk, was also beavering at test essays. There was also a practical element; a man was sent down from the institute to witness a trial lesson.

Well, I did it. I took the papers, passed, survived the trial lesson, and duly received my diploma. Fine. Object achieved.

Some months later, I received a letter from a young man who told me that he too had it in mind to take the post-grad. certificate exams. He said he had met a colleague of mine who had told him what I had done, and would I be kind enough to write to him and give him some kind of guidance as to how to go about it.

This I did. Nothing happened.

Months later again, I received a letter from him at last. In it he said how grateful he was for my help (and apologised for the delay). He said he had just taken the exams and was awaiting the results.

'I don't think I really did enough to prepare sufficiently, and I don't know whether I have passed. But it doesn't matter, because I have just been offered a job as a senior lecturer in education at a teacher training college.'

A job not just as an ordinary teacher, please note. Nor even as a lecturer in a teacher training college. But a *senior lecturer*. And in *education*.

How do you follow that?

Arise, Sir Sir

IF YOU LAY DOWN the law about anything, no matter how well-qualified and well-informed you may be, it is a fair likelihood that you will receive salvoes of criticism and disagreement, not to say correction, possibly even outright abuse. If you venture to make any observation on something about which you are *not* well-informed, you should stand by for being not merely corrected but shot down in flames.

I am about to venture into such a minefield (if you can be shot down in flames in a minefield).

Have you ever wondered what rewards are available for teachers? Apart from promotion, that is. And there's not much of that. Not like the Armed Forces, where you can proceed right up the scale of ranks to the dizzy height of Field Marshal or Admiral of the Fleet (not much chance of that either now, with the whole Navy down to 30,000 men). No young probationer carries a Minister of Education's baton in his knapsack. Indeed, if he wants that sort of promotion, the sooner he leaves the profession the better. Rather like the state of affairs among the clergy – if you want a bishop's mitre, you don't stay in parish pastoral work, do you? You don't even start in it. It is the same with politicians: if you want ministerial rank, you don't beaver away knocking on doors in rural constituencies or licking envelopes in local party headquarters; you get a job as an 'adviser' to a leading politician in Westminster.

Note – the common factor seems to be that if you want to get to the top of a particular profession, you must give up the practice of it as soon as possible.

On Teaching

Look at teaching. If you stay in it, you can become a head of department, then a deputy head, or maybe a director of studies, and finally of course a headmaster. And that's about it.

What about money? I don't think anybody has ever set out a case for the huge financial rewards that teachers can aspire to. Nobody in his right mind who wants to make 'serious' money would dream of entering the classroom. In any case it is a truism – well, we hope it is – that young people do not enter the profession with the profit motive uppermost in their minds. And a good thing too.

Not much in the way of public recognition either. When did you last hear of a respected teacher being asked to open a civic centre, or present the prizes at a county show, or launch a major charity initiative? They just don't get noticed. Well, not if they are in the classroom anyway. Yes, I know all the adverts say that 'nobody ever forgets a good teacher'. True. But, when it comes to dishing out the rewards, nobody (well, hardly anybody) *remembers* a good teacher either.

If they do get the MBE or the OBE or whatever, it is usually for something he or she has done, in addition to their teaching, *outside* the classroom.

Now that is curious. A rugby player will get the MBE for winning the world cup; he won't get it for scores of coaching sessions held in boys' clubs. A jockey doesn't get his award for pioneering revolutionary medical treatments for racehorses; he gets it for winning races. An athlete gets his for jumping into a sandpit, not for appearing on chat shows for charity. Even a lollipop lady will get her gong for being just a lollipop lady, not for making kilograms of damson jam for the local church bazaar for twenty years.

All these worthy and successful ladies and gentlemen get their award for doing their thing, not for doing other things.

One hears of a handful of teachers who have actually been awarded knighthoods, but when you look more closely, you discover that they were those wonderful supermen (and women) who 'turn round' failing schools. They got them for being great organisers and leaders and administrators; they didn't get them for giving super lessons in Biology to the middle stream for thirty-five years.

So – to repeat – I have never heard of a case of a classroom teacher being given a knighthood for his work *in the classroom*. Stanley Matthews got his for his wizardry on the right wing for Stoke City and Blackpool. Bradman got his for being the greatest batsman alive. Gordon Richards got his for being the most successful jockey in England for over twenty years.

And so they should have. They worked at it all their professional lives, and they fully deserved their distinction. But a teacher can slave away at theorems or experiments or grammar exercises all *his* working life, and be acknowledged by all those who know him to be the greatest since Jesus or Socrates – I have never heard of *his* getting one.

Now – always assuming I am right, and this is where I must expect the flak – why should this be?

Once upon a time, knighthoods were awarded for prowess on the battlefield, which was only natural. It was where most men could come to the attention of their sovereign. Later, as government became more, shall we say, settled, knighthoods could be, and were, awarded for distinguished service of another kind, usually in the field of government. Mostly 'establishment' figures, note. But that was to change.

Now and again, a gifted, or very lucky, outsider would do something so remarkable that a sovereign would employ knighthood as a very convenient way to reward him. (Note I say 'him'; it was a man's world until well into modern times. I have no idea when the very first 'Dame' was created.) So if you sailed round the world or captured India or smashed the French Fleet, you got your knighthood.

That too changed, or rather was extended, half-way through the twentieth century, when, to the surprise of many, and possibly the chagrin of many more, they decided to give knighthoods to *sportsmen*, of all people. Dash it all, wasn't this lowering the currency value? What was the world coming to?

It was coming to pop stars, that's what. And variety performers, film stars, actors, TV presenters, almost anybody. So, despite what the Old Guard might think or say about Lowering Standards (and sending back their own gongs when the Beatles got their MBE's), we are now truly democratic; you can get a knighthood for anything. Except, it seems, for labouring in the galleys of middle-school Maths for nearly forty years, and being adored by generations of pupils, who can count among their number seventy-four MA's, fifteen Ph. D's, two archbishops, a Foreign Secretary, a member of the Order of Merit, and a Nobel Prizewinner.

One is tempted to wonder whether the establishment – the faceless bureaucrats, the *éminences grises*, the men in grey flannel suits, the Humphrey Appleby's of this world – somehow 'have it in' for teachers.

Or rather, perhaps, that they have *nothing* 'in' for teachers. Sportsmen, say, attract admiration nearing hero-worship, and maybe the knighthood-awarders are to a certain extent guided, or pushed, in that direction by public adulation or the media. Popes are fond of maintaining that they do not create saints out of nothing; they do it because of the existing adulation of the Faithful. They are not leading; they are following. The same could apply to actors, and other performers in the public eye.

Certain professions have always commanded respect. Doctors, for example. They preside over life and death, they are privy to knowledge way above our heads, they work minor miracles with their drugs and their operations. No doubt, along with the respect, goes a modicum of fear, even dread. We all hope that we can stay out of their clutches for a very long time.

Lawyers too, with their wigs and their tortuous byways of the law, can baffle us, trip us up, get us off, and generally make a great deal of money, and we all hope once again that we are not on the receiving end of an extended cross-examination, or caught up in Byzantine litigation which only lawyers understand and which only lawyers profit from. But one rarely hears of a serious campaign to lower lawyers' fees or dignity. Their behaviour is a mystery, and, as a general rule, we like mysteries.

Then too, there is the technique of getting one's rewards written into the contract right at the outset, so that they (the rewards) become not only expected, but inevitable. In the Civil Service, we are told, the MBE's and the CMG's and the KCMG's and GCMG's come up with the ration truck. So there is no argument and no debate – just a scale.

But the teaching profession is different. Part of the reason for this may be the fact that we have all been to school. We have all had lessons from teachers. We have watched them close to, and seen all the warts. They don't wear fancy wigs and throw Latin phrases around to describe what they're doing; they don't punch us full of holes and pour awful drugs into us. We have all been taught, so we all know everything there is to know about education. We know damn all about medicine or the law.

Teachers are ordinary, all too ordinary and all too human. And they can, in our memory, be held guilty of years of boredom and bullying. We see them under pressure, and we see their weaknesses. When we deal with doctors and lawyers, we are the ones under pressure, not them.

Quite possibly, the same applied to the priesthood, in the days when every community had a parson or a minister or an elder. It goes way beyond awe. They didn't punch us full of holes or blind with and torts and malfeasances; no – they could scare us half to death with threats of Hellfire. They could preach to us – and did – about our sins, which we, and they, knew all about, and which they could bring out into the light every Sunday morning from the pulpit.

Teachers simply do not have that sort of clout.

I have often wondered whether this does not go right back to ancient history. There have always been priests and doctors and lawyers – if you like, one of the unavoidable results of 'civilisation'. They all soon developed their own mystique and their own professional secrets and their own freemasonry, and their own machinery for their self-perpetuation.

Teachers, on the other hand, began as slaves. The ancient world was built on slavery. In a society with very little technology, human labour had to do what machines did not exist to do at that time. Slaves were plentiful, and they were dirt cheap. In fact, free – by definition – because you never had to pay them. Only feed and house them.

So, when wealthy family men decided that an education would help their sons in the world, they turned, very naturally, to the resources nearest at hand. Most of them would have an educated slave or two. If they didn't, it was a simple thing to go out and buy some. And you handed over your children to them. No doubt many of them made a very good job of it.

But the fact remained that they were slaves. A slave teacher might be given the authority to drum things into pupils' heads, to drive them, to bully them, even to beat them, but the fact remained that they were still slaves, and the pupils knew this.

Now, times changed over the centuries, and proper schools gradually emerged (this is a ridiculously inadequate way to summarise two thousand years of education history). But did there still remain, deep down, that sense of humble beginning which continued in people's attitude to the teaching profession?

In other words, is it fair to suggest that people simply do not take the teaching profession as seriously as they do the medical profession, or the legal profession, or the gentlemen of the cloth? Or, come to that, law enforcement, the prison service, and all the huge organisations which represent millions of employees in a host of 'humbler' activities. A strike of doctors, or miners, or train-drivers, or prison staff, might give a few sleepless nights to the relevant ministries and their civil servants, but I have never heard of a teachers' strike toppling a government, or even causing much more than a wrinkle in a ministerial brow.

So – is there a lesson to be learned here for teachers? If we want some brilliant, or devoted, or successful classroom practitioners to be suitably rewarded with distinctions on the same level, and with the same frequency, as in other professions, we shall have to make the teaching profession as strong, as united, as mystique-ridden, as deserving of respect, as they are. Not necessarily nicer – rather perhaps a bit more spiky, cussed, bolshy, confident, above all sure of their worth.

Just as an electorate are said to get the governments they deserve, is it too controversial to suggest that teachers also get the rewards they deserve, and that they won't get any more till they do something about it?

Some progress made

THE ONLY LESSON TO be learnt from history is that there isn't any lesson. Well, that's what some historians say. By the same token, the only moral to be gleaned from this account of my 'career' is to accept that there isn't one there either.

Take a look at the figures. Nine months in the first school job; twelve months in the second; eleven years in the third; sixteen in the fourth; and thirty years in the fifth. It is an odd progression to say the least.

I had never wanted to be a teacher in the first place. 'Trouble was, I had never wanted to be anything much – anything, that is, which offered a means of support. I thought I must be a bit peculiar. I fancied myself as a writer, yes, but even I was sufficiently practical – just – to accept that, in the meantime, Something Had to be Done. So I cannot lay any claim to a vocation.

Nor can I claim that, once embarked in the classroom, I set about Building a Career. The first job was only a temporary contract. I obtained the second because I was the only candidate for it. I was offered the third because I knew the headmaster, or rather he knew me, and it saved a lot of short-listing and interviewing. The fourth came along because the headmaster there had just been let down by a sixth-form teacher at the very last minute, and he was right up against it. I just happened to be around. The last one came about because, again, a colleague who knew me suggested me to the headmaster – only as a part-timer. I don't think either I or the headmaster imagined a long tenure. I certainly did not; I said to myself that I would give it a term just to see how it went.

After about ten or twelve years, 'it' showed signs of drying up. I thought – not for the first time – well, that was that. Then, within a very short time – along came an offer from this headmaster: would I care to set up a school archive?

Well, it was that or the sack, so I said, 'What a splendid idea.' I was not troubled by trivial matters like gaping lack of experience, paucity of knowledge, or total absence of professional qualifications. Neither, it seemed, was the man who made the offer.

I said to him, 'How would you like me to run it?' He said, 'Any way you like.'

It was straight out *The Godfather*, wasn't it? An offer I couldn't refuse.

That was twenty years ago. Put that with the years I spent teaching there, and it comes to thirty, in a school where I said I would 'give it a term'. You would have a job to find a moral in that.

Happily for me – if not for my readers – I am pleased to say that, in amongst it all, I did manage some writing after all.

THE END

www.ingramcontent.com/pod-product-compliance
Lightning Source LLC
LaVergne TN
LVHW051544070426
835507LV00021B/2401